leading
the discipleshift

becoming a **disciple-making church**

brandon guindon // lance wigton // luke yetter

foreward by jim putman

NAVPRESS
Discipleship Inside Out

Discipleship Inside Out®

NavPress is the publishing ministry of The Navigators, an international Christian organization and leader in personal spiritual development. NavPress is committed to helping people grow spiritually and enjoy lives of meaning and hope through personal and group resources that are biblically rooted, culturally relevant, and highly practical.

**For a free catalog go to www.NavPress.com
or call 1.800.366.7788 in the United States or 1.800.839.4769 in Canada.**

© 2013 by Branden Guindon, Lance Wigton, and Luke Yetter

ISBN-13: 978-1-61291-495-4

DiscipleShift by Jim Putman and Bob Harrington © 2013 Zondervan.
Cover images by Veer, iStock, Getty, Masterfile, and Photo.com

Some of the anecdotal illustrations in this book are true to life and are included with the permission of the persons involved. All other illustrations are composites of real situations, and any resemblance to people living or dead is coincidental.

Printed in the United States of America

1 2 3 4 5 6 7 8 / 18 17 16 15 14 13

Contents

foreword

Brandon Guindon, Lance Wigton, and Luke Yetter have not only been a part of an amazing God adventure at our church, they have been used by God to help make needed changes over the years to an organization that has stalled many times.

Change is inevitable if we are to continue to grow as Christians, and the same is true of churches. The landscape is filled with empty buildings that were once needed for thriving congregations. When they decided that it was better to be comfortable than to walk in faith as God led, then they began to die.

Not only have these men helped us change over the years, they have helped hundreds of churches change as well.

If true change is to happen, we must have the right destination and the right plan to get to the right destination. Many great leaders have led thousands to the wrong destination and thus ended up failing. Others have had the right destination but did not lead in the right way, therefore had no one follow them to the right place. Either way it's failure. We must lead to the right place in the right way if we are to succeed.

Leading people to a relationship with Jesus and to becoming disciples who can make disciples is the right destination. Leading in such a way that people feel valued, motivated, and a part of something they understand and deem important enough to give their life away for is to lead in the right way.

These guys can help you think through both of these issues and help you and your church become a light in your community as a result. I am proud of them and to work alongside them.

Jim Putman
Senior Pastor of Real Life Ministries
Author of *Real-Life Discipleship, Real-Life Discipleship Training Manual,* and *DiscipleShift*

a word for facilitators

The Bible is full of stories about change. Abraham changed his home address (to put it mildly), David changed his occupation, and Saul/Paul changed his allegiance. One of the strongest, however, is the story of Nehemiah. Nehemiah was faced with the daunting task of rebuilding the wall around Jerusalem and needed to rally the entire nation for the massive job that lay ahead. He knew that to pull this off he needed the Lord's help but also a workforce that believed in what needed to be done. They had to have clear leadership, communication, and an understanding of the end goal. He had to change a group of people who were beaten, broken down, and in some ways completely lost. He would lead them in a way that resulted in buy-in and commitment to the end goal. He celebrated the victories along the way and with God's help and direction they shifted the course of an entire nation.

How do we lead change? That question appears at the center of most conversations we have with church leaders. Most pastors/leaders we talk to agree there are problems in the church and see that some shift needs to happen. Whether a pastor from a hundred-year-old church in the Bible belt or a young leader from a relatively new church plant, leading a church through change can be similar to what Nehemiah faced—a daunting task. This workbook is designed to help you not only look at how to lead change, but also and even more importantly, what you are leading people to shift.

What Do I Need?

To effectively go through this book we strongly recommend that you go through this experience with your lead or core team—a group that together will lead the church through change. Gather a group of four to eight people who will lead the change. We call this group your "key influencers" or your immediate team. You will need to set time aside for personal investment in this workbook, much like a devotional. Also, set a consistent time to meet once a week as a group to review the previous week's material.

What Can I Expect?

We will walk you through the what and the how of leading change. Often Christian leaders will recognize a problem but lack the road map to help them reach the end goal. The approach becomes "Ready, fire, aim!" The person or group launches in a direction with no strategic plan or clear target. They just begin making changes without thinking them through and without having a clear understanding of the impact. At Real Life Ministries we have certainly made that mistake, and we want to share with you what we have learned. You can expect exercises, stories, and practical examples that will help you to lead change and focus on the right target.

How Do I Use This Workbook?

Each lesson will challenge you to look not only at your church, but also at your own personal leadership skills and experiences. We are going to encourage you to look within yourself and investigate ways to grow as a leader that will in turn help the church as a whole. On the fifth day of each week we have provided a group format. You will use this day to facilitate discussion among your leadership team. Together you will process the key points and new ideas you have explored. We challenge you to examine yourself and be honest with your team. This workbook will definitely be one of "those" exercises: you will get out of it what you put into it. So prepare your heart and mind to dive in and begin asking (and answering) some tough questions. The questions that will help you navigate may be the most important shifts your church needs to make so that you personally and corporately effectively impact God's kingdom.

How Do I Not Use This Workbook?

We ask that you do not begin implementing changes while going through the book. Do not parallel path the change with your progress through the book. Go through the whole book before you implement anything. Trust the process! Often leaders want to begin "doing" the change before "being" the change, but this will cause confusion and communication breakdown. Trust us on this!

Facilitating this group is a great responsibility. Much of this workbook is written from the perspective that you have read (or will read) the Real-Life Discipleship Training Manual. That resource will give you a deeper understanding of terminology and concepts of the discipleship process we are going to revisit. This workbook is designed for your higher levels of leadership to help shift your church to a place where discipleship is an integral part of the culture.

We would also encourage you to establish some group rules before beginning. To help you do that, we have included on the next page a group sheet to talk through and sign as an indication of each individual's commitment. In general, you'll want to set your group norms, such as when you meet and how often. We recommend that you meet for two hours once a week. To effectively process all the information and grow in your relationship together, you must dedicate time.

What Materials Would You Recommend That I Read or Have Available to Complete This Workbook?

To navigate through this workbook it is not mandatory that you have completed other materials by the RLM team, but again it will help. Of course, the Bible is essential to have available as you work through the exercises.

- The Bible
- *Real-Life Discipleship Training Manual* by Jim Putman, Avery Willis, Brandon Guindon, and Bill Krause
- *Real-Life Discipleship* by Jim Putman
- *Church is a Team Sport* by Jim Putman
- *DiscipleShift* by Jim Putman and Robert Coleman

What If There Are More People Wating to Go through the Workbook Than I Can Fit in My Group?

This is a common question we get. We recommend that you actually have several teams from your church going through this material at the same time. At the end of the workbook you will put together an action plan. Creating separate action plans and then comparing and combining them to generate one plan is a great way to create powerful buy-in to the change in your church.

preparing for your first meeting

Before you begin the study, it is important to have a "pre-meeting" with the people you've chosen to take this journey with you. The preliminary meeting will give the group an understanding of the risks and rewards associated with this commitment to begin moving your church toward change. Some of the discussion will force the group to simply agree on details such as when and where you'll meet. Before the meeting ends, you'll ask your group to make a commitment to God and each other.

Facilitating the First Meeting

Begin with a brief time of vision-casting and clearly communicate with the group why they have been personally selected for this team. Distribute *Leading the DiscipleShift* workbooks for each member, explaining the general format of four days of individual, devotional-style exercises and a fifth day for you to gather as a group for a time of discussion built on each week's assignment. It is vital to the success of not only these group meetings but also for this season of preparation for God's fresh movement that everyone be fully and prayerfully engaged personally and in group discussions. Remind group members to take their time and avoid rushing through the daily sessions or cramming them into a last-minute study session before the group meeting. Everyone will need to be prepared to discuss a primary takeaway from each day. Allow time for the information in each carefully crafted day to marinate and mature, fully soaking in, so that the group time is a natural overflow of leaders who have immersed themselves in God's Word and the practical principles saturating the pages of this workbook. (As the facilitator, you will want to be sure to highlight or make note of points and questions from each day's exercise for group discussion during the weekly review.)

Explain that during your group time together over the course of the next eight weeks, you will begin each meeting with a time of prayer and reflecting on biblical principles revealed in the narrative of Nehemiah. Group members may choose to read through the entire book (only thirteen chapters) this week before your next meeting if they prefer having the big picture in mind as they then work step by step through the process of leading God's people to focus their lives on a unified purpose.

Take time as a team to read Nehemiah 1:1-4.

Nehemiah led God's people through a transition that not only altered their lives, but also impacted the culture of the time and for generations to come. Like many biblical leaders, Nehemiah exercised great wisdom in practical matters of strategic planning, foresight, management, delegation, and casting vision. But excellent leadership was not enough for Nehemiah. Nor is it enough for God's leaders today. A fiercely devoted relationship with God, humbly following the Lord's guidance, as well as boldly and sacrificially putting ourselves on the front lines to see God honored and His work accomplished are paramount.

The psalmist rightly declared, "Unless the Lord builds the house, the builders labor in vain. Unless the Lord watches over the city, the guards stand watch in vain" (Psalm 127:1).

The goal of this workbook is to honestly assess what God has called us to do as leaders, what He is calling you to do specifically among His people in your unique context, and to respond to His unchanging Word with integrity and faithfulness.

Too often leaders rush into things, with either practical know-how or biblical truth, thinking good intentions are enough to make up for the missing other side to the coin. God has called us to be both faithful stewards of His truth and responsible stewards in the day-to-day "business" of ministry.

Since each week's group discussion will begin with prayer and a select passage from the book of Nehemiah, you'll want to highlight the following reminders in your preliminary meeting to "introduce" this biblical leader:

- *Nehemiah was a real man at a real point in history. His story is not merely inspirational; he successfully led a major shift in his culture. Our task is to lead God's people today.*
- *Nehemiah asked about and cared about God's people. What God opens our eyes to may be affirming what we intuitively knew, or we may be surprised to learn things are different than anticipated.*
- *Nehemiah's response and starting point must also be ours—hitting our knees in prayer and burying our faces as we cry out to heaven, brokenhearted for the condition of God's people and the desperate need for change.*

Following Nehemiah's example, encourage your leadership team to pray and fast this week, eagerly seeking God during this critical season. Then conclude this introductory session with a time of corporate prayer in whatever fashion seems appropriate. It would be ideal for each person to voice a short prayer and to determine what he or she will set aside in fasting during this week or this entire study in order to gain practical wisdom and to focus intently on hearing from and replying to God in prayer.

Group Questions and Commitment

Because you believe God has called you as a leadership team to make changes, with the Lord's help you will begin this journey together. To get started on the right foot, go through the following questions and share your responses.

leading the discipleshift – preliminary meeting

PRACTICAL INFORMATION

What day and time will the group meet?_____

Who are the members of the group (first and last names)?

_____   _____
_____   _____
_____   _____
_____   _____
_____   _____
_____   _____

Gut-Check Questions

What is your greatest fear about leading change in our church?

_____
_____
_____
_____
_____
_____
_____
_____

What are you most excited about for our church when the change begins to be implemented?

_____
_____
_____
_____
_____
_____
_____
_____

What do you expect from the others in this group while you go through this workbook together?

_____

_____

_____

_____

_____

_____

_____

What do you commit to doing for the group as you journey through the workbook?

_____

_____

_____

_____

_____

_____

At the end of the workbook, what do you hope happens within this group and our church?

_____

_____

_____

_____

_____

_____

_____

MAKE A COMMITMENT!

As a group we have made the commitment to the Lord and each other to work together to learn how to walk out healthy change for our church body. I agree with and commit to the others in my group. As evidence of this commitment, I will sign below.

_____   _____

_____   _____

_____   _____

_____   _____

_____   _____

foundational definitions

This first week is the groundwork for everything that follows. Laying this foundation will require a little extra focus to dig into some vital concepts, so allow yourself as much time as necessary to thoroughly and honestly reflect on each day's questions. Day 1 will ask a lot of questions to give you the opportunity to assess what God has for the church He has entrusted to your leadership—not to prescribe a generic formula from what "worked" in one church to "remedy" another.

We will briefly touch on the importance of relationship as defined from God's perspective, and how important relationship is for advancing His church. Also, we will assess where you are currently with making disciples, valuing relationship, and creating healthy environments. Remember, it starts with you! Then, finally, we will look at what you might need to change personally and corporately.

From what we see today, many churches are not sure why they exist. They continue to carry on the traditions of what their church has "always been." But typically people coming to know Jesus is not a regular occurrence. Leaders are often scarce and new leadership has to be hired from outside the local church body.

What did you relate to when you read the above paragraph describing the church today?

_____

_____

_____

_____

_____

_____

_____

_____

Day 1

WHAT IS THE PURPOSE OF THE CHURCH?

Before we even begin to look at shifting anything in the church or considering any change that may be required, we need to thoughtfully and honestly answer some foundational questions.

In what areas of your church are you experiencing spiritual growth?

_____
_____
_____
_____
_____

How are you seeing Jesus transform people daily? Weekly?

_____
_____
_____
_____
_____

What are you measuring to help you and your team know that God's kingdom is advancing through your church?

_____
_____
_____
_____
_____

Are the measurements you listed above things Jesus measured? If so, what Scriptures speak clearly to this measure or definition of discipleship?

_____
_____
_____
_____
_____

If your church was no longer here, would it be missed by the community? If so, why?

_____
_____
_____

_____

Does your church have a statement of vision/mission/purpose? Does your church have core values? If so, write them here (from memory).

_____

What connection do you see between the stated mission and values of your church and any of your answers above to disciple-making and measures of "success" or growth?

_____

From what you see, why consider a shift in the direction, organization, and/or focus of your church? Why do you have a burning desire to see change in your church today?

_____

Are you satisfied with your church's current state of disciple-making, or do you want more for God's people? Why? (Be prepared to share this answer with your teammates in the group discussion session at the end of the week.)

_____

What is the purpose of Jesus' church?

As we've worked with different churches across the globe, we've noticed one common issue: a lack of clarity of vision. It's not just that churches are drifting from their vision; that would imply that they understood it at one point and have moved away over time. No, many churches aren't even sure what they're supposed to be doing—let alone *how*.

Not having a clear biblical vision and direction for God's church oftentimes results in chaos. Imagine a quarterback calling a play in the huddle, but his teammates don't even know why they are on the field or worse yet, how to even win the game. Many believers are having to guess at the purpose of God's church based on what they see on the weekend, and that leaves them to draw one conclusion: the purpose of God's church must be for its members to come and listen to a good sermon. Not that a good biblical sermon is bad, but how does that bring clarity to the purpose of the church for the whole congregation?

Let's avoid the guesswork and get the purpose of the church from Jesus Himself. What did Jesus say was the "greatest" commandment? (See Matthew 22:37-40 and Mark 12:29-31.)

If you are living out the above commandment, what is your identity? How will you be known? (Read John 13:34-35.)

What did Jesus say to His church shortly before He returned to heaven? What purpose did He give them? (See Matthew 28:18-20.)

Making disciples of Jesus is not a twenty-first-century concept or merely a buzzword as the latest trend in contemporary Christianity. It is the commandment Jesus gave us to obey. So we must recapture His priority as our priority. Jesus not only gave us a message to share, but He gave us a method and a model for making disciples. Churches today have focused on the message and overlooked the method He modeled.

Making disciples is the natural result of loving God and loving others. Making disciples is not another program added to the church's busy schedule.

Focus Exercise

What would you say is the purpose of Jesus' church?

_____
_____
_____
_____
_____
_____
_____

What would your congregation say? How would they finish this sentence?
"Our church exists for the purpose of

_____
_____
_____
_____
_____
_____

It might be a good idea for you and your team to randomly ask your congregation, "What is the purpose of our church?" Then compare your findings to help assess your people's understanding of this topic. Asking good questions to get reality on the table is a critical skill a leader must be willing to develop.

Also, making changes in the corporate body begins with you. Over these next several weeks you will be challenged to reflect on yourself, your team, and the body of Christ prior to making any changes.

Many leaders want to skip looking at themselves and go right to fixing the team and the body of Christ. However, leading change well begins with you the leader modeling the changes you want to see. After all, it's much easier to follow someone who is living out his or her own advice. Amen?

Day 2

HOW DO YOU MEASURE SUCCESS?

Did yesterday's questions help to shift your attention toward the chasm that exists between the church Jesus called us to be and the corporate church that exists today? By participating in this study, you are preparing to lead change in your church body. We believe God is calling His church to recognize how far we have strayed from the biblical model. We believe God is calling church leaders to notice and take ownership of the gap that has been created between how people currently define discipleship and how Jesus modeled discipleship. These gaps should drive us to our knees.

Jesus' Church

First, let's look at what Jesus said about His church. Read Matthew 16:18 (in the margin) and then fill in the blanks to the statement below

1. The _____ of _____ will not _____ Jesus' church.

And I tell you that you are Peter, and on this rock I will build my church, and the gates of Hades will not overcome it.

(Matthew 16:18)

You should have written gates, Hades, and overcome. In this passage Jesus made a very important claim. He said that "His" church will overcome the gates of hell. So when we look at our own city, state, nation, or even across the globe, do we see the church prevailing against the gates of hell?

2. Place an X next to the statement you believe best describes the church prevailing.

_____ 1. We have built an amazing thousand-seat auditorium.
_____ 2. Our Sunday school classes have all memorized the book of Philippians.
_____ 3. Our church financially supports ten missionaries around the world.
_____ 4. Our church has small groups where people are being challenged to know each other and know God on a deeper level.

Auditoriums, memorizing Scripture, and supporting missionaries are all great things. We want Christian people to know the Lord and be givers so that the kingdom advances throughout the world. What Jesus modeled with His life here on earth was a relational kind of ministry. God's heart is that we know Him and each other on a deeper level. Through that relational growth we would then reach out to others. Jesus's church prevails when relational fruit is being produced both corporately and individually.

3. Read John 17:20-23. Place a T next to any statement you believe is true and an F next to any statement you believe is false.

A. _____ The world will come to know Christ if we solely focus on our walk with God.
B. _____ The church will prevail by just being in community with each other.
C. _____ The world will be drawn to Christ by seeing our unity and love for each other.

D._____ The church must remain in a close relationship with Christ as well as with each other.

E. _____ The relational components of discipleship are irrelevant.

In the statements above, only C and D are true. The church prevails when the church body remains unified in relationship because that unity becomes a light to the world. They see our care for each other and are drawn to it. Discipleship is the process of our growing in relationship with Christ and others.

Was Jesus Wrong?

Statistically we know the church overall is struggling. In fact, in some areas of the world, like the United States, the church is losing dramatically and the gates are very much prevailing. What does this mean, then, in regard to the claims of Christ?

- 1. Jesus is wrong.
- 2. Jesus is a liar.
- 3. The church has stopped being Jesus' church.

Hit Your Knees

If we really believe Jesus is God, then options 1 and 2 are impossible. Option 3 is the answer. The church has stopped being Jesus' church in many ways. We certainly are not saying that all Christians today are going to hell; what we are saying is that the church has lost its direction and changed what "winning" is. Leaders have bought into a win for church that Jesus never said was victory. Anything outside the success Jesus defined for His church is broken. We must take ownership of the brokenness, as a sinful man would own his sin. As leaders in Jesus' church, we must own this gap, this chasm.

We see consistently in Scripture that when God's people are confronted with their sin and separation from Him there is a process of confession and repentance. This attitude taps into the heart of God that we do not often experience as a twenty-first-century church.

How have you as a leadership team led your church in the past when God convicted you corporately of misdirection?

4. Below check the box or boxes that best apply.

- ☐ We have never considered this idea of a corporate repentance.
- ☐ When we see misdirection we create new programs to attempt to solve the problem.
- ☐ We appoint a committee or a board to investigate and solve the problem.
- ☐ We ignore it.
- ☐ We gather together as a leadership team and seek God for help and confess our loss of focus.

My prayer is not for them alone. I pray also for those who will believe in me through their message, that all of them may be one, Father, just as you are in me and I am in you. May they also be in us so that the world may believe that you have sent me. I have given them the glory that you gave me, that they may be one as we are one—I in them and you in me—so that they may be brought to complete unity. Then the world will know that you sent me and have loved them even as you have loved me.

(John 17:20-23)

I prayed to the Lord my God and confessed: "Lord, the great and awesome God, who keeps his covenant of love with those who love him and keep his commandments, we have sinned and done wrong. We have been wicked and have rebelled; we have turned away from your commands and laws. We have not listened to your servants the prophets, who spoke in your name to our kings, our princes and our ancestors, and to all the people of the land. "Lord, you are righteous, but this day we are covered with shame—the people of Judah and the inhabitants of Jerusalem and all Israel, both near and far, in all the countries where you have scattered us because of our unfaithfulness to you. We and our kings, our princes and our ancestors are covered with shame, Lord, because we have sinned against you. The Lord our God is merciful and forgiving, even though we have rebelled against him; we have not obeyed the Lord our God or kept the laws he gave us through his servants the prophets. . . . Lord, in keeping with all your righteous acts, turn away your anger and your wrath from Jerusalem, your city, your holy hill. Our sins and the iniquities of our fathers have made Jerusalem and your people an object of scorn to all those around us.

"Now, our God, hear the prayers and petitions of your servant. For your sake, Lord, look with favor on your desolate sanctuary. Give ear, our God, and hear; open your eyes and see the desolation of the city that bears your Name. We do not make requests of you because we are righteous, but because of your great mercy. Lord, listen! Lord, forgive! Lord, hear and act! For your sake, my God, do not delay, because your city and your people bear your Name." (Daniel 9:4-10, 16-19)

It is much easier to put a task list together and send your team out to start "doing" the change, but knocking out a list of items and assignments can be done by anyone. Taking ownership of the flaw, our sin, and repentance before the Lord is something else. Before you as a group do anything else, own and repent. That's where the "doing" begins. For your team to move forward, confession and repentance is key.

Right now ask God to reveal specifically what your church leadership team should repent from.

5. In list A write the things God places on your heart.

LIST A

_____

_____

_____

_____

_____

_____

6. Read Daniel 9:4-10, 16-19. Underline the key phrases that model how to approach corporate confession and repentance.

You should have underlined phrases like "we have sinned and done wrong…;" "We have not listened…;" "we have not obeyed …;" "turn away your anger." This passage shows clearly the attitude Daniel modeled. An attitude of acknowledgment, ownership, and brokenness is what the Lord seeks from those who stray.

7. In your small group, compile (in list B) the items you agree represent the specific things God is calling you as a team to confess and repent of. Take both of these lists (A and B) to God and ask for forgiveness.

LIST B

_____

_____

_____

_____

_____

_____

Hunt the Right Animal

When I (Brandon) was in high school my dad, grandfather, and I went elk hunting, as we often did in the fall. This trip was different than the others because we had invited a new friend. He was our neighbor, and we were glad to have him along. After an hour or so we reached our hunting destination. It was dark, early in the morning, and, as I remember, exceptionally cold. As each of us collected our gear and slung our rifles, my dad laid out the basic plan of the morning hunt. Off we went, hunting one of Idaho's most wonderful game animals. Several hours into the hunt, just down the hill below me, I heard a shot fired. It didn't sound like a typical, big-game, large-caliber rifle shot, though. As I immediately began to process what I had just heard and figure out where exactly it had come from, someone cried out, "I got one! I got one!" Rushing over to investigate what sounded like the voice of our new hunting partner, I was shocked by what I didn't see. There was no downed elk, but with a huge smile on his face, our neighbor held in his right hand his gun and in his left his trophy: a tree squirrel. The gun I had heard was a .22. No wonder I never heard the loud crack of the typical large-caliber gun that would take down an elk. Our new friend had created all this commotion and ruined the morning hunt—all over a tree squirrel! I couldn't help but think, *How in the world could you have thought we were hunting squirrels?*

We reflect on that story because there are parallels to what we see in the church today. This new friend's idea of what "winning" was for the day was not at all what the rest of us thought. Somewhere the goal was not clear or had been totally lost. In fact his goal, which he was so proud of, actually ruined my goal. In his mind the day was a total success; in mine, utter failure. How could two hunters have such massively different goals?

8. List some key concepts that you think contributed to the failed hunt that day.

_____

_____

_____

_____

_____

_____

_____

Therefore go and make disciples of all nations, baptizing them in the name of the Father and of the Son and of the Holy Spirit, and teaching them to obey everything I have commanded you. And surely I am with you always, to the very end of the age.

(Matthew 28:19-20)

You should have written concepts such as lack of communication, no clear goal, assumed ideals and goals, and so on. This problem plagues the church today, and so often encourages church leaders to hunt for the wrong goals. Then, when they reach those goals, they learn their co-leaders were not on the same page.

In our other books and workbook, *Real Life Discipleship,* we talk a great deal about what winning is. Read Matthew 28:19-20. Circle the concept below that best states what Christians are called to do:

Evangelize the lost ** Preach the Word ** Care for the hurting ** Make disciples of Jesus Christ ** Fight over the color of the carpet ** Debate the gifts of the Spirit ** Open political debates on Facebook

So often the goal of the church is to do good things. We should reach lost people and care for the hurting as well as preach the Word, but all of that falls under the umbrella of the Great Commission.

9. Reflecting on today and yesterday, write out some of the good things your church does.

_____
_____
_____
_____
_____
_____

10. As objectively and honestly as possible, define in one sentence what winning is for your church.

_____
_____
_____
_____
_____
_____
_____
_____

11. On the scale below place an X that represents how far away you believe your church direction is from the mandate to "go and make disciples" in a relational environment.

●——●

off the map   cold but trying   getting warm   on target   we're there

12. Now go back and look through your answers from questions 3, 4, and 5. If your church continues on its current course for the next ten years, what will have been accomplished?

_____
_____
_____
_____
_____
_____

So, if the purpose of the church—and therefore our measure for "success"—is to make mature disciples, we'll need a clear definition of *disciple.* Tomorrow we will seek to establish such a definition.

WHAT IS A DISCIPLE?

Day 3

Desalegn, a Christian brother in Ethiopia we work with, is a powerful leader. God has used him to lead significant change in the evangelical church in Ethiopia. Like the Western church, Ethiopia has strayed from the biblical model of discipleship. They too have generally defined "winning" for the church as levels of attendance and biblical knowledge. In a meeting with many of the country's highest level leaders, Desalegn made a profound statement. He said,

We have lost our focus, we have strayed. Our churches have lost direction. At one time in our country we faced persecution, and the church was forced to rely on relationship with God and each other because we had nothing else. Now we do not know each other. We only focus on sermons and singing music. Lives are not changing, and they are very shallow. The church has lost Jesus' method of making disciples. We must return to His ways!

1. Place a checkmark next to the statement below that best represents your response to Desalegn's statement:

_____ Strongly agree
_____ Somewhat agree
_____ Neutral about the statement
_____ Disagree
_____ Strongly disagree

2. Why did you choose the statement you did? (Be prepared to discuss this with your group.)

_____

_____

_____

_____

_____

_____

We said yesterday the purpose of the church—and therefore our measure for "success"—is to make mature disciples. So, what is a disciple? And what did Jesus say about it?

Let's think about it this way: Do you love people enough to be in relationship with them in order to share the gospel? Well, sharing your life with them doesn't stop with you leading your neighbor to Christ. We are called to make disciples, not converts.

The discipleship process doesn't stop when people accept Jesus as their Lord and Savior. It doesn't even stop when they "get involved in church" (depending on what is meant by that statement). New Christians need help growing and developing in their walk. They need someone to walk beside them—someone who is more mature and can help them figure out what this new journey looks like. This goes way beyond showing up on Sunday or even memorizing Bible verses. And guess what? You can't do it all. So, now what?

Are you personally called to disciple everyone on the planet? Or are you called to make disciples who can make disciples, thus ensuring God's people get disciple? Jesus discipled only twelve, but look at what the Holy Spirit did with their efforts. We are here today because disciples modeled what Jesus did with them. They made disciples of Jesus, who made disciples of Jesus. Everyone who has Jesus as their Lord and Savior should be making disciples of Jesus. Have you ever been told that you are to go and make disciples? Have you ever told the people you're leading that they are to be disciple-makers of Jesus?

3. What comes to your mind when you think of being a disciple of Jesus? What does that mean to you?

_____

_____

_____

_____

_____

4. Read Matthew 4:19. How did Jesus describe a disciple?

_____

_____

_____

_____

Jesus called His disciples, and they actively responded by following Him. Jesus said He would make them into something new; they were agreeing to be transformed by Him. Jesus's invitation specifically says that He would make them fishers of men; they were committed to His mission.

Committed to _____ Him;
Committed to being _____ by Him;
Committed to His _____.

The above is a possible definition you could use for a disciple of Jesus. (We say a "possible" definition because this is the one we here at RLM have agreed to use. You might choose to use it, or you might choose to come up with your own. Either way, the important thing is you have defined the term.)

Below are some of the criteria we used to help us define what we mean by disciple. The definition had to be

- Biblical
- Easily understood and memorable
- Clear enough to enable us to celebrate being and making disciples. It's great to help people see they are being and/or making a disciple of Jesus so they don't have to guess (something we will discuss in greater detail in week 7). As Scripture says, "Encourage one another daily" (Hebrews 3:13).

Clarity on the Win

In no way are we suggesting that any church copy Real Life Ministries. What we are saying is that we hope you copy the model from Scripture.

Matthew 4:19 has provided us with a clear definition of a disciple that can be used several ways. A clear definition of a disciple helps leadership aim for the same target and provides the church body a more precise point of unity. Consistently at RLM our staff and volunteer leaders wanted to know what was expected of them and if we were (and are) accomplishing the win together. Like any organization, we had to begin with a clear definition that then enabled us to better communicate vision, mission, and even focus in our trainings.

Below is a list of areas in which we suggest you speak or print the definition of a disciple so your church body hears or sees it regularly:

- Membership classes
- Yearly leadership classes
- Sermons
- Bulletins
- Website
- Leadership rallies/vision-casting retreats
- Banners in the foyer
- Individual ministry announcements

5. What is your a definition of disciple? (Be prepared to discuss your definition with the group.)

_____

_____

_____

_____

_____

As a group, discuss and agree upon a definition of a disciple. Record that definition below. Remember to keep it biblical and practical.

_____

_____

_____

_____

_____

_____

Today you narrowed down the purpose of Jesus' church. You have begun to bring clarity to the definition of a disciple. The impact these two things will have on your church is massive. When the church aligns itself with one vision and people start pulling together for that purpose, it will give the church a tremendous amount of momentum. Great job!

Day 4

HOW IMPORTANT IS RELATIONSHIP?

Having worked with Christian leaders from across the world, we've seen one thing that notably propels them forward or holds them back from advancing God's kingdom: relationship.

Jesus said, "Go and make disciples of all nations, baptizing them in the name of the Father and of the Son and of the Holy Spirit, and teaching them to obey everything I have commanded you. And surely I am with you always, to the very end of the age" (Matthew 28:19-20, "Emphasis" added).

Many church leaders broadcast truth from a platform and expect people in an audience to obey. Others emphasize comfort and belonging in community, while shying away from much expectation for obedience. So, how important is relationship when it comes to teaching and obedience? If discipleship is about spiritual growth, can we expect people to mature in obedience without relationship? Consider this scenario: As a parent, how important is relationship when it comes to getting a teenager to obey? Circle the one you feel best describes your answer:

Not Really Important	Somewhat Important	Important	Very Important	Critically Important

Here's a simple equation to keep in mind when it comes to relational value.

RULES – RELATIONSHIP = REBELLION.

Read John 14-15. How important is relationship according to Jesus?

Not Really Important	Somewhat Important	Important	Very Important	Critically Important

1. What phrases jump out as relational in John 14-15 in the description of the connection between teaching (truth/words/commandments), obedience (faithful/fruitful living), and relationship?

_____

_____

_____

_____

_____

_____

_____

Write the Ten Commandments below (Exodus 20:1-17). As you read each one, ask yourself, does breaking this commandment affect relationships?

1. _____
2. _____
3. _____
4. _____
5. _____
6. _____
7. _____
8. _____
9. _____
10. _____

Is there a single commandment that is not relational?

Fill in the fruit of the Spirit (Galatians 5:22-23) in the blanks below. These qualities are defining characteristics of a healthy and mature disciple. Every quality is relational.

_____ with whom?
_____ in whom?
_____ with whom?
_____ with whom?
_____ toward whom?
_____ toward whom?
_____ toward whom?
_____ with whom?
_____ helps or hinders relationship with whom?

Bonus exercise: Would you say Jesus modeled a high value on relationships? Where do you see that in the Scriptures? List some examples.

_____
_____
_____
_____

If relationships are vital (and they are), how do we encourage real-life relationships instead of merely programming groups or activities to attend?

The Relational Environment

In our first workbook, *Real-Life Discipleship Training Manual,* we spent extensive time on defining relational environment. Relationships may well be the most sought after yet most absent piece in the discipleship journey. To lead a true DiscipleShift, clarity on the relational environment is essential for the church. Without true relationships and a healthy environment in which to nurture them, discipleship cannot be successful.

Creating a Relational Environment

First let's clarify the absolutes for a relational environment. The relational environment is the vehicle that we travel in to get to the destination. A relational environment is not the destination. Small groups are essential to create the relational environment because the necessary characteristics cannot happen in a large group.

Read the statements below and check the box next to the statements that indicate a healthy relational environment.

- ☐ Everyone in the group is being open and honest with each other.
- ☐ The group helps take care of each other's needs outside of the group.
- ☐ When someone is missing from the group, people call to check on them.
- ☐ There are open discussions and people can ask the leader questions to help process biblical truth.
- ☐ New people are welcomed and invited in.

Each of these statements are key components of a relational environment. When we look at God's nature we can see that He is relational. Scripture is filled with examples of God expressing His nature in a relational way and the relationship that He desires for us to have with each other.

3. Read John 17:21; Acts 2:42, 46-47; Romans 13:9; Romans 15:1; and Hebrews 3:13. Underline the key statements the writers made about our relationships with each other. Compile those concepts and write your own statement about a relational environment.

_____

_____

_____

_____

_____

In order for your church to create healthy relational environments, you as a leadership team must recognize the areas of weakness that exist. To lead change you need to have a clear idea of the components of the relational environment so you can correct the shortcomings.

4. What key characteristics need to be added within your church so you are more relational overall?

_____

_____

_____

_____

_____

_____

[Insert in the margin: ...That all of them may be one, Father, just as you are in me and I am in you. May they also be in us so that the world may believe that you have sent me.

(John 17:21)

They devoted themselves to the apostles' teaching and to fellowship, to the breaking of bread and to prayer. . . . Every day they continued to meet together in the temple courts. They broke bread in their homes and ate together with glad and sincere hearts, praising God and enjoying the favor of all the people. And the Lord added to their number daily those who were being saved.

(Acts 2:42, 46-47)

The commandments, "You shall not commit adultery," "You shall not murder," "You shall not steal," "You shall not covet," and whatever other command there may be, are summed up in this one command: "Love your neighbor as yourself."

(Romans 13:9)

We who are strong ought to bear with the failings of the weak and not to please ourselves.

(Romans 15:1)

But encourage one another daily, as long as it is called Today, so that none of you may be hardened by sin's deceitfulness.

(Hebrews 3:13)

5. Your leadership team casts a shadow over the whole church body. If that shadow could talk, how would it describe itself relationally? Finish this statement: Relationally, we are _____

_____

_____

_____

_____

_____

6. To dive in and really understand the key relational environment characteristics you'd like to see in your small groups and church body, complete the following statements:

I feel safe in a small group when _____

_____

_____

_____

_____

_____

The behavior that convinces me people care is _____

_____

_____

_____

_____

_____

_____

People seem authentic when they treat me like _____

_____

_____

_____

_____

_____

Asking questions of a leader is important to me because _____

_____

_____

_____

_____

_____

_____

_____

If I could have two characteristics in a small group, they would be _____

_____

_____

_____

_____

_____

_____

_____

7. Write a summary based on how you answered the statements from question 6. Discuss this summary in your small group._____

_____

_____

_____

_____

_____

_____

8. In your small group, create a unified statement that describes the essentials of a relational environment. Try to put Scripture to each component. _____

_____

_____

_____

_____

_____

_____

_____

REVIEW AND GROUP DISCUSSION

Day 5

Pray

Following the pattern of Nehemiah's example, humbly confess that though God has placed you in a position of leadership, you are ultimately His servant. Be bold in asking for success and His favor as you seek to follow His will, revealed by His Word and through His Spirit at work among you and His people.

Scripture

Choose a group member to read Nehemiah 1:1-11.

Key Points

- (1:3) A problem was identified. Gaps existed between what should be, what once was, and the current reality surrounding God's people. Consequently, distress filled the community.
- (1:4) Nehemiah began by recognizing the need, allowing himself to feel the heart-breaking weight of the burden, and then praying and fasting for "several days." This was where we also officially began last week.
- (1:6-7) The power of "we" is introduced in the opening lines of this story. Collective responsibility is vital not only to leading change, but also in recognizing our own part in the current state of things. A godly leader acknowledges his or her own part as part of the community—it is not just a "them" problem. Nehemiah included himself in his corporate prayer of repentance and asking for God's favor.

After spending the past week in study, prayer, and fasting, we are going to now identify the "gaps" we see in our church and the resulting distress in our community.

The Week In Review

Discuss the major points and questions of each day, revisiting anything you may have marked throughout the week for group discussion. Share honestly about where God is challenging and encouraging you. Make sure your group environment is one of mutual respect, tempering observations and responses with grace. Time will not allow you to discuss all the questions, but visit the milestones and make sure each group member has an opportunity to offer input.

Day 1: What is the purpose of the church?
Day 2: How do you measure success?
Day 3: What is a disciple?
Day 4: How important is relationship?

Personal "Shifts" As a Disciple

What is God teaching you about Himself? About yourself? About this church?

Week 1 Takeaways

What key truths, principles, and/or insights will you take away from this week's experience?

Action Steps

What action steps will you prayerfully consider based on this week's experience? Remember, be patient to let God fully develop your action plan. Resist the urge to jump into action immediately. You will revisit these in week 8 to formalize a clear plan of action for leading the *DiscipleShift* within your context.

Setup for Next Week

Now that we've established some foundational understandings, created working definitions, and identified potential gaps between God's design for His church and our current reality, we'll begin to look more specifically at five components and shifts in disciple-making. These are pillars upon which a healthy, long-term ministry strategy can be built in any context.

five components and shifts in disciple-making

I (Brandon) love a great, hearty stew! In my family a specific recipe has been passed down for four generations. Both my mother and grandmother would say the process of making the stew is as important as the ingredients. I cannot help but draw the correlation between this family tradition and discipleship. In the coming week we are going to focus on the ingredients of the stew, or the five components that we see in discipleship.

For you to lead the *DiscipleShift* (or any change) in your church, you must know what you are leading toward. This week we'll spend time clearly outlining for you the components of disciple-making as we see them in Scripture. Of course, we cannot (and wouldn't even try to) put disciple-making, the work of the Holy Spirit, in a box. We are, however, applying language and some structure to help you create change and find a clear direction to lead your church.

Day 1

BIBLICAL FOUNDATION AND SHIFT #1—
From REACHING to MAKING

The entire discipleship journey has a biblical foundation. For you to lead change and create an authentic disciple-making church, you must look to the Bible for direction.

What do you think having a biblical foundation for discipleship means?

_____

_____

_____

_____

_____

_____

Self-Evaluation

Rate yourself from 1 to 5 (1 being "almost never" and 5 being "all the time") on how regularly you look to the Bible for truth and direction in the following areas:

_____ Personal relationships (marriage and friendships)
_____ Parenting
_____ Personal financial practices
_____ How to make life decisions about your present or future
_____ How to disciple a person God has placed in your life

How did you do? Do you have areas you know need to move up the scale? Many of us do, especially if we believe the Bible is the Word of God and our final authority for how to handle life. Many pastors often miss the fact that the Bible gives us a clear picture on how to disciple someone. The Bible gives us a foundation for all of life's circumstances.

So when we talk about a biblical foundation for discipleship, this is how we define it: **Biblical foundation**—*The Bible alone gives a clear and complete picture of what God wants done (His mission) and how He wants it done (His methods). All other components of disciple-making are coming from this perspective.*

Comparison

Does your definition agree with or differ from ours? Write out any major differences you see.

_____

_____

_____

_____

_____

_____

Doing Some Research

What key biblical stories or Scripture passages would you use to begin building a case that making disciples of Jesus is a biblical concept? Spend some time in Bible study, and then list the verses below.

Below you will find an exercise to add to your work. You may have even come up with some of the same verses.

Connect the verses to the basic phrase that illustrates important aspects of discipleship by drawing a line from the Scripture verse to the numbered statement. This will help you see that making disciples is a biblical concept and that we can point directly to the Scriptures for guidance.

Matthew 28:19	1. We must be committed to it.
Matthew 4:19	2. Relationship is important.
2 Timothy 2:2	3. We are commanded to do it.
1 Thessalonians 2:8	4. We will be changed by it.
Luke 9:23	5. We are called to pass it on.

Your answers should have been a-3, b-4, c-5, d-2, and e-1. This simple exercise shows that what we do when making disciples is based on a biblical foundation. In your church, how could you go about establishing a clear connection for your people pertaining to disciple-making?

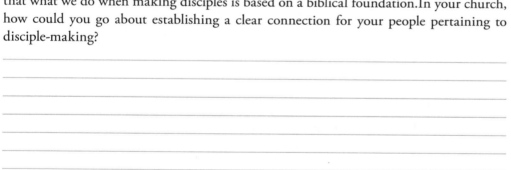

▶▶ SHIFT #1: *From Reaching to Making*

The Biblical Purpose of the Church

Let's be honest. Reaching people is simple. All you need is a great marketing technique and a venue that is pleasing to the masses. Then entertain like nobody's business so they keep coming back. But if just reaching people were what Jesus called us to do, then He would have modeled it like this: He would have done a few miracles (marketed Himself then told those people to go tell everyone), picked a place that was well known and extravagant

Then Jesus was led up by the Spirit into the wilderness to be tempted by the devil. And after fasting forty days and forty nights, he was hungry. And the tempter came and said to him, "If you are the Son of God, command these stones to become loaves of bread." But he answered, "It is written, 'Man shall not live by bread alone, but by every word that comes from the mouth of God.'" Then the devil took him to the holy city and set him on the pinnacle of the temple and said to him, "If you are the Son of God, throw yourself down, for it is written, 'He will command his angels concerning you,' and 'On their hands they will bear you up, lest you strike your foot against a stone.'" Jesus said to him, "Again it is written, 'You shall not put the Lord your God to the test.'" Again, the devil took him to a very high mountain and showed him all the kingdoms of the world and their glory. And he said to him, "All these I will give you, if you will fall down and worship me." Then Jesus said to him, "Be gone, Satan! For it is written, 'You shall worship the Lord your God and him only shall you serve.'" Then the devil left him, and behold, angels came and were ministering to him.

(Matthew 4:1-11, ESV)

(Caesar's palace), preached from a platform wearing a robe of gold, and had His disciples preaching "back-up." He would have stopped right there and moved on to His next venue, hoping the "information" stuck well enough so they would return next time He preached. He might have reached a lot of people, but what would have become of those people? Would He have made disciples or fans?

I really don't think any of that is the picture we have in our minds when we think of what Jesus did here on earth with His disciples or with His people. Or is it? How do we, our leadership, and our congregation picture making disciples?

Driving as many people into the building as possible is a common church goal. Unfortunately the long-term impact is a lot of people looking for a better Sunday worship service to keep them entertained.

How would you describe how well your church leaders (elders, executive leadership, staff, key volunteers) understand the purpose of the church (to make disciples of Jesus)?

_____

_____

_____

_____

_____

_____

How passionate are you about making disciples of Jesus? How do you measure your passion?

_____

_____

_____

_____

_____

_____

Give three reasons why it is important to have a basic definition of a disciple of Jesus. (Be prepared to share this answer with your group.)

1._____

2._____

3._____

What ministry in your church is the closest to aligning with the church's purpose of making disciples of Jesus? Why did you choose that particular ministry?

Jesus was tempted with shortcuts, spectacle, crowds, and influence; but He remained faithful to the Word of God and the life-changing mission of God. As His followers, we're expected and empowered to do the same.

Day 2

INTENTIONAL LEADERSHIP AND SHIFT #2—
From INFORMING to EQUIPPING

Most people never think about "being intentional." As I (Brandon) grew up in northern Idaho, my dad taught me a great deal about hunting elk. We spent hours in the woods together (and still do). When I was a young boy he intentionally taught me about reading the terrain, knowing animal tendencies, and understanding general animal behaviors. This investment allowed me over the years to build a strong understanding of important hunting principles. Most importantly I learned a strong love for God's creation.

1. Think of a hobby or sport that you enjoy. How did you learn that activity? Who taught it to you? What specifically did that person do to teach you that activity?

_____

_____

_____

_____

_____

_____

Think about the intentional things that happened so you could learn that activity. Maybe there was modeling or verbal instruction. Most likely you had to practice and have someone watch you or critique your form.

2. What are you intentional about? Consider your hobbies, sports, work, marriage, parenting, and so forth.

_____

_____

_____

_____

_____

How did you do? Are you an intentional person? Modeling one of the keys of disciple-making, that Jesus was incredibly intentional with the disciples. Based on how Jesus discipled, we would argue that no one can make a true, healthy disciple of Jesus without being exceptionally intentional. So, to make sure we are using the same language, let us first define what we mean by intentional leader.

Let's Define It!

Intentional Leaders: Leaders who invest in the lives God entrusts to them. They actively and purposefully partner with the work of the Holy Spirit in the lives of others. They understand where a person is spiritually and what is needed to help that individual grow.

When we look at the life of Jesus, we can see many instances in which He was incredibly intentional.

3. Read the story of the feeding of the five thousand from John 6:1-14. List ways Jesus was intentional.

_____

_____

_____

_____

_____

_____

You hopefully saw things like Jesus planned, He knew what He wanted to accomplish, He was teaching the disciples, He cared for the needs of the people, He involved His disciples in His plan.

When we look at this story we can see that Jesus had a plan (John 6:6 says He clearly had in mind what He was going to do), and He wanted to intentionally use His disciples. Our best example is Jesus, so we imitate Him.

Read the observations listed below. Think about them as they pertain to your life as a follower of Christ.

- Many willing Christians have absolutely no plan for disciple-making.
- Nothing about the life of Christ was haphazard.
- Jesus had an end goal and knew what He was leading them toward. His goal was not merely education, although He educated.

Jesus' process was intentional but not rigid. He did not control every possible situation. He was flexible. He met people where they were and yet did not compromise the end goal.

4. How does your life align with the statements above? What would you like to see change?

_____

_____

_____

_____

_____

Jesus understood what was at stake. He knew the game.

Read through the following observations. Think about them as they pertain to your life as a follower of Christ.

- Intentional leaders must understand the game. We are in a spiritual war.
- An intentional leader is trying to teach and equip someone else to "play the game."
- Christians are often unaware of the spiritual war.

After this Jesus went away to the other side of the Sea of Galilee, which is the Sea of Tiberias. And a large crowd was following him, because they saw the signs that he was doing on the sick. Jesus went up on the mountain, and there he sat down with his disciples. Now the Passover, the feast of the Jews, was at hand. Lifting up his eyes, then, and seeing that a large crowd was coming toward him, Jesus said to Philip, "Where are we to buy bread, so that these people may eat?" He said this to test him, for he himself knew what he would do. Philip answered him, "Two hundred denarii worth of bread would not be enough for each of them to get a little." One of his disciples, Andrew, Simon Peter's brother, said to him, "There is a boy here who has five barley loaves and two fish, but what are they for so many?" Jesus said, "Have the people sit down." Now there was much grass in the place. So the men sat down, about five thousand in number. Jesus then took the loaves, and when he had given thanks, he distributed them to those who were seated. So also the fish, as much as they wanted. And when they had eaten their fill, he told his disciples, "Gather up the leftover fragments, that nothing may be lost." So they gathered them up and filled twelve baskets with fragments from the five barley loaves left by those who had eaten. When the people saw the sign that he had done, they said, "This is indeed the Prophet who is to come into the world!"

(John 6:1-14, ESV)

5. How does your life align with the statements above? What would you like to see change?

_____

_____

_____

_____

_____

_____

Intentional leaders create an environment for growth. Read Ephesians 4:11-14. Our job as leaders is to equip!

▶▶ SHIFT #2: *From Informing to Equiping*

And he gave the apostles, the prophets, the evangelists, the shepherds and teachers, to equip the saints for the work of ministry, for building up the body of Christ, until we all attain to the unity of the faith and of the knowledge of the Son of God, to mature manhood, to the measure of the stature of the fullness of Christ, so that we may no longer be children, tossed to and fro by the waves and carried about by every wind of doctrine, by human cunning, by craftiness in deceitful schemes.

(Ephesians 4:11-14, ESV)

The Methodology and the Role of the Leader

I (Brandon) love watching fishing shows where they *inform* me about their techniques, what they used to catch that "big one," and all about their successful trips. But, boy, when the rubber hits the road and I'm out there trying to catch the big one myself, I may be reflecting on what I heard during that show, but what I really wish is that I could have spent time with those guides, watched them up close and personal, asked questions along the way, and then tried out their techniques within the safety and comfort of their boat. How much better my trip would have been had I had some hands-on *equipping*? So, you may not be called to be a fisherman, but we are all called to ministry. The same concept of informing and equipping applies to us.

Informing: Telling somebody, communicating information or knowledge to somebody.
Equipping: Providing somebody with necessities, providing somebody with what is needed to succeed in a particular activity or role in life.

I can inform somebody all day long with knowledge, but if I want him to use that information to succeed at something then I must be willing to walk alongside him, learn what he as an individual requires to succeed, and then provide him with the necessary tools. Even going so far as to help him hone those tools as he moves forward. Education is a great thing. By itself, however, without the heart and hands of equipping, information isn't necessarily all that practical.

Shifting from Informing to Equipping

When it came to making disciples, did Jesus inform His disciples of many things? List at least five things Jesus informed His disciples about.

1. _____

2. _____

3. _____

4. _____

5. _____

We all would agree that informing/educating is a vital part of discipleship, but is that all Jesus did? How did He intentionally equip His disciples for ministry beyond informing them? Think of one biblical story and list some key ways Jesus equipped His disciples.

_____

_____

_____

_____

_____

_____

As a leader for the kingdom, you have influence. What you believe gets lived out in your actions, and those actions impact others around you. Would you agree? Yes or NO?

Do you see yourself as someone who tends more to inform or as someone who tends more to equip? Support your answer with examples from your life and ministry. (Be prepared to share this with your group.)

_____

_____

_____

_____

_____

_____

Do you see your church as more of an informing church or more as an equipping church? Support your answer with examples from your ministry. (Be prepared to share this answer with your group.)

_____

_____

_____

_____

_____

_____

What key elements are needed for a person to be equipped? Or, if you prefer to think of it in a different way, if you were to take on a totally new role, what are some vital elements you would need to feel equipped?

1. Would you want to know the overall purpose of your new role?
2. Would you want a place to practice the new skills required to excel at this role?

3. How would you want to be treated when you failed as you were trying something new?
4. How important would encouragement be to you during this process?
5. How important would it be to know ahead of time the dos and don'ts in this new role?

6. Would it be important for the person who is equipping you to model what the role looks like and be willing to spend time with you?

_____
_____
_____
_____
_____
_____
_____

Look at the questions above from two perspectives. First, from Jesus' perspective. Was Jesus intentional about equipping His disciples? How did He do as an equipper? How do you know?

_____
_____
_____
_____
_____
_____
_____

For the second perspective, imagine someone asking people on your team those questions about you and your equipping. What would they answer?

_____
_____
_____
_____
_____

What would people on your team say are your strengths as an equipper?

_____
_____
_____
_____
_____

What would people on your team say were "over strengths" of your equipping? (Over strengths are strengths that are turned up too strong, can be overdone, and actually hinder your ability to equip and relate to others.)

_____

_____

_____

_____

_____

What can you specifically pray about and ask the Lord to help you with to become a better equipper?

_____

_____

_____

_____

_____

_____

_____

_____

Day 3

RELATIONAL ENVIRONMENT AND SHIFT #3—
From ACTIVITY to RELATIONSHIP

Jesus often used an organic model to teach and bring clarity to people following Him. Today we also will look at the needs of a plant to illustrate the importance of a healthy relational environment.

Every gardener wants healthy plants that produce and grow. To have a healthy plant, certain elements must be present: soil, water, and sun. If even one of these elements is not present, the plant will not grow into maturity. However, we as good gardeners would never settle for anything less than healthy growth. We understand our responsibilities—to continually evaluate these elements and make necessary changes immediately. We also know that God and His creation will cause the seed to grow with these elements present into something really fantastic.

Like plants, we as Christians need certain elements in place to help us grow in our relationships with the Lord and other people. Just as a plant's environment is essential to its growth, so, too, Christians require an appropriate environment—a relational environment. Without it, we will not thrive. Within that relational environment three essential elements provide what believers need to help them grow and mature: time, truth, and love.

Time

Jesus modeled for us the importance of spending time with a small groupS of people when He gathered twelve and focused on three. He demonstrated small group for us as future disciple-makers because it is the only method that works. Many excellent preachers have felt they were able to lead the entire congregation by preaching on Sunday. Preaching and casting vision from the pulpit is important. Jesus also thought it was important; He often preached to the masses that gathered. However, Jesus also spent time with individuals, His disciples, shepherding them and investing in them. To encourage a person to grow and to model maturity for someone, you must spend time together—which can only happen with just a few people. Jesus didn't have kids and email to answer and phone calls to make. However, even the Creator of the universe and the greatest disciple-maker ever limited distractions and focused on His twelve. Jesus modeled for us effective discipleship and how to live a balanced life by gathering twelve and focusing on three.

Time with a few gives the people you are in relationship with access to see you model what it looks like to be a Christian. When times are tough, how do you respond? What happens when there is conflict with others? What topics are consistently hot buttons for you? How do you apply Scripture to daily living? You can't experience the answers to those questions in a classroom. It takes time.

How do you need to modify your schedule to make more time available for the people you are discipling?

_____
_____
_____
_____
_____

What impact—both positive and negative—might those changes make?

_____
_____
_____
_____
_____
_____

Truth

Jesus spoke the truth no matter who He was talking to—the inquisitive woman at the well, His disciples, the antagonistic Pharisees. Jesus always responded with the truth no matter how difficult or unpleasant. Many of us tend to steer away from giving our perspective to others because we're concerned it might not be the truth; it might be just our perspective and we don't want to hurt anyone. We justify withholding truth from others by misusing the biblical principles of humility, peacekeeping, and bearing with others.

Sanctify them by the truth; your word is truth.

(John 17:17)

The reality is when we speak the truth we actually make the environment a healthy and safe place for others to grow. Imagine avoiding telling a two-year-old to stay out of the street, because you didn't feel like it was your place! The same applies when we are dealing with adults who are still spiritual infants. Even if our statement is only our perspective, bringing it into the light will only strengthen the relationship in the long run as we relationally work through the issue. Jesus had multiple documented conversations with many different groups. Regardless of the situation and risk, Jesus was able to insert truth into the discourse.

What are truth are you withholding from people you are in relationship with? What would the impact be if you acted like Jesus and told them the truth?

_____
_____
_____
_____
_____
_____

Love

Going back to our gardening analogy, you'll remember the element of sunshine is crucial to plant life and growth. Imagine trying to plant in the dead of winter! No matter how much effort you put into the other parts of gardening, nothing would grow and you would be wasting your resources. The same is true in your relational environment; it simply falls apart without love. Love must be the central part of discipleship and relationship. Far too often leaders talk about discipleship as something they are going to "do" to someone—as if discipleship is a program or training.

Discipleship is who you are. The people you have chosen to disciple are the people you love. If you don't above all else love the people in your relational environment, then it will eventually fall apart.

However, if love were all your entire relational environment had going for it, it still might work! Think of the people you know who love you, regardless of any situation or circumstance. Don't you value what they value? Don't you care about what they care about?

Do you really love the people you want to disciple? Knowing that people don't care how much you know until they know how much you care, what is the impact if your answer to the first question is no?

_____

_____

_____

_____

_____

_____

If I could speak all the languages of earth and of angels, but didn't love others, I would only be a noisy gong or a clanging cymbal. If I had the gift of prophecy, and if I understood all of God's secret plans and possessed all knowledge, and if I had such faith that I could move mountains, but didn't love others, I would be nothing. If I gave everything I have to the poor and even sacrificed my body, I could boast about it; but if I didn't love others, I would have gained nothing.

(1 Corinthians 13:1-3, NLT)

▶▶ SHIFT #3: *From Activity to Relationship*

The Vehicle—Relational Small Group

In today's society we are certainly never at a loss for things to do. Between family and household obligations, work, a multitude of extracurricular activities, and the constant barrage of technology and media, we can fill our days and nights indefinitely.

So why as the church do we tend to add more activities, ministries, to-dos, and "Christian tasks" to our plates? We certainly do not see Jesus walking around with His calendar of events and His to-do lists and then fitting in His disciples and discipleship into vacant spots. His disciples were a major priority. He spent intentional time with them, doing life with them and discipling them every step of the way. He modeled, He equipped, He aligned, He was with them relationally. In other words, He provided a relational environment.

This environment consisted of a small group of men who over time were encouraged, loved, cared for, and rebuked (in love). And "then Jesus came to them and said, 'All authority in heaven and on earth has been given to me. Therefore go and make disciples of all nations, baptizing them in the name of the Father and of the Son and of the Holy Spirit, and teaching them to obey everything I have commanded you. And surely I am with you always, to the very end of the age.'"

If we are obedient to God's Word by going and making disciples, then following His method as well makes the most sense. Small-group relational environments are necessary to achieve the Great Commission.

However, it doesn't stop there. As Jesus said, "And surely I am with you always," we must continue to build those relationships, not necessarily with the same amount of time we did at the beginning, but as the body we remain in relationship for eternity.

Think about the different ministries, events, and activities your church and leadership maintain and have scheduled. Are they consistent with Jesus's method of small-group discipleship?

_____

_____

_____

_____

_____

_____

What would have to "shift" for them to look more like a small-group environment? (Keep in mind, any shift usually has to start with leadership.)

_____

_____

_____

_____

_____

_____

How could you gauge whether you are being relational in these endeavors?

_____

_____

_____

_____

_____

Which activities are relational versus activities that occur simply for the activities' sake?

_____

_____

_____

_____

_____

Thinking back to the previous days and using those principles, describe what an intentional ministry might look like in its disciple-making process. (Incorporate aspects from each day, starting with day 1.) Reflect on these three questions to help you with your description:

1. If Jesus were here today (and you didn't know He was God), would you hire Him onto your staff? Would His pace and attitude fit with your culture? Why or why not?

_____

_____

_____

_____

_____

_____

_____

2. Does your church as a whole value activity and getting stuff done more than valuing relationship and investing in people? Why? (Be prepared to share your explanation with the group.)

_____

_____

_____

_____

_____

_____

3. Do the activities in your personal schedule align with making disciples the way Jesus modeled (time spent, doing life together, being friends, investing, equipping, helping His team to understand the Word, and so on)? In the left-hand column, list the activities that align with what Jesus modeled. In the right-hand column, list those that don't line up.

Activities in Alignment	Activities Out of Alignment
_____	_____
_____	_____
_____	_____
_____	_____

(Be prepared to share your aligned and unaligned activities with your group.)

REPRODUCIBLE PROCESS AND SHIFT #4—
From ACCUMULATING to DEPLOYING

CHURCH ALIGNMENT AND SHIFT#5—
From PROGRAM to PURPOSE

Day 4

We continue this week talking about the importance of the five elements of being a disciple-making church. The last two are reproducible discipleship process and alignment.

Reproducible Process

Most simply, a reproducible discipleship process is a method for developing people toward maturity in Christlikeness. This includes three parts: the discipler's part, the disciple's part, and God's part. Consider spiritual growth to be similar to human development. If we recognize a person's maturity level, we have right views of responsibility, capability, and needs that person may have. The needs and abilities of an infant are far different from those of a child, teenager, young adult, or mature adult. This is true not only physically and socially, but spiritually as well. Our goal is to recognize a person's maturity level, adjust our expectations to match that level, and encourage the person to grow up. (This is discussed in detail in *Real-Life Discipleship* and the *Real-Life Discipleship Training Manual.* If you are not familiar with the discipleship process described in *Real-Life Discipleship* and *Real-Life Discipleship Training Manual,* we would suggest pausing this workbook process and going over that until you and the rest of your group feel comfortable with the information. It is truly the lifeblood of the church body.)

Physically and spiritually, life is passed on as people mature and reproduce. The goal of our churches should not be to function as spiritual nurseries where we spend all of our time keeping needy infants happy and comfortable, judging success by the amount of whining we hear. The church is a family that's intended to grow, share responsibility, and multiply. This should happen naturally and in any environment. It shouldn't be dependent upon gathering people into a building or program, but releasing the DNA of Christ followers into the world to be fruitful and multiply, filling the earth with His likeness.

▶▶SHIFT #4: *From Accumulating to Deploying*

As parents, we know that we are to raise our children to the best of our ability, equipping them to leave our home someday and go on to raise up their own children. Why is it that we can apply that concept to our families, yet when it comes to ministry and raising up disciples, we sometimes forget to release them once we've raised them up? Why is it that when we really should be stepping aside and allowing them to lead the next small group, or minister to the next person who walks into our benevolence ministry, we tend to hold on to that position? We aren't supposed to be accumulating "troops" but never releasing them to fight.

Shifting from accumulation to deployment often creates a struggle within the leadership of a church and can ultimately end up causing division. There is no official "test" that can be given during the disciple-making process to determine if a person is fully qualified to be released. There is no human measuring stick that we can hold up to one another to see if we have met the requirements.

However, we can rest easy in knowing that God used people such as Matthew, Thomas, Peter, Paul—men who by human standards were not qualified to do God's work. Whether they did not hold the correct occupation, they were seriously doubting Jesus, or their past sin was just too much, when they were held up to the human measuring stick, they didn't cut it.

Now, don't get us wrong. We need to equip and align disciples just like Jesus equipped and aligned His disciples before He sent them out. But once we have done our part, we have to trust God to do His part and release people to do their part.

Let's look at some important alignment values that drive the deploying philosophy. Doing so will help you to think through both your church's and your personal values of deployment.

Alignment Values that Help in Building a Deploying Philosophy

On a scale of 1 to 5 (1 being "not a value for me/us" and 5 being "this is part of who I am/ we are"), rate yourself and your church on the following value statements:

I (we) create a place to play. My (our) environment is a place where others can serve and be part of the body, a place for them to get into the game.

Rate yourself: 1 2 3 4 5
Rate your church: 1 2 3 4 5

It's okay to fail. It's important to make efforts and attempts, and it's okay not to do it perfectly.

Rate yourself: 1 2 3 4 5
Rate your church: 1 2 3 4 5

All parts of the body are needed. All gifts and abilities are valued, and my (our) exact way of doing things isn't the only way of doing things.

Rate yourself: 1 2 3 4 5
Rate your church: 1 2 3 4 5

Get into the game. I'd (we'd) rather be involved than sit on the sidelines. I (we) understand I (we) stretch and grow when I (we) play.

Rate yourself: 1 2 3 4 5
Rate your church: 1 2 3 4 5

I am (we are) not my (our) work. Negative or positive feedback is not taken personally. My (our) work is God's work, and He gets the credit.

Rate yourself: 1 2 3 4 5
Rate your church: 1 2 3 4 5

Alignment

This last step is definitely the most difficult of the five components. Alignment involves everyone in a church, and it should never be considered accomplished. Imagine you are driving a huge bus that is carrying every man, woman, and child who is part of your church. As the bus driver, you get the bus headed toward your destination. You would never then consider taking your hands off the wheel and hoping the bus arrived safely at your destination! You know you will make continuous, slight adjustments to the steering wheel the entire time you're driving. You're going to have to make other driving adjustments as well, depending on the weather and terrain, the needs of the passengers, and road conditions.

The same goes for alignment of the church toward the destination of making disciples. You and the church leadership need to be vigilant and unified to align the entire church in four key areas: relational, organizational, theological, and philosophical.

Relational Alignment

How do individuals within your culture relate to each other? How do the people celebrate and care for one another? Most of these interpersonal interactions are nonverbal and understood from a collective frame of reference, usually a shared experience or many generations of shared experiences. Sometimes leaders struggle to see the forest through the trees, especially if leadership has been together in one place a long time.

Relational alignment is making the entire group aware of the strengths and weaknesses of the culture. Moving together toward the culture being able to disciple each other and anyone who might join in the future. Changing directions in this area is difficult and feels very awkward at first, but small changes toward relational health can make a huge impact. For example, you could meet with two or three friends just to have fun, or have a meeting where you don't feel the need to teach or have an agenda but just want to see what is going on in each other's lives.

But if we are living in the light, as God is in the light, then we have fellowship with each other, and the blood of Jesus, his Son, cleanses us from all sin.

(1 John 1:7, NLT)

What relational norms is the leadership of the church communicating to the congregation? Are they healthy and aligned with what Jesus modeled? Are they using examples of what is going on in their small groups? Are they talking about challenges they are overcoming for the sake of relationship? Bragging about people they know and the growth toward spiritual maturity they are making? Give some specific examples.

_____

_____

_____

_____

_____

_____

_____

Organizational Alignment

If your church is dedicated to making disciples above all else, the church should have the budget, staffing, and calendar to support making disciples. We are not suggesting that you don't pay the heating bill because it doesn't directly impact making disciples. We are, however, suggesting that leadership carefully assess expenditures and strategic decisions to make sure they align with making disciples as efficiently as possible.

If a consultant were to look at your church's budget, calendar, and staff positions, would the person easily conclude that leadership values discipleship? What evidence would support his or her conclusion?

_____

_____

_____

_____

_____

_____

_____

_____

Theological Alignment

Getting people to align on their theology is crucial to growing as a disciple-making church. For the purpose of unity in the future, new people must fully understand the church's stance on theological issues. The church needs to agree on its "no compromise" issues as well as its "this is what we believe but we don't expect everyone else to necessarily agree with us" issues. Not being aligned on theology can easily strain relationships and hurt spiritual infants. It is up to church leadership to bring clarity to these topics for the sake of unity.

What would be the impact if a home group started asking questions and the leader's answers didn't align with the church's theological statement?

_____

_____

_____

_____

_____

_____

_____

Philosophical Alignment

The statement your church has on its wall in the foyer may be called a vision statement or a mission statement. Regardless of its name, the statement has to be aligned with making disciples of Jesus. This is important because many ministry leaders and volunteers make decisions and focus their collective energy toward that one statement.

Can your church leaders and volunteers correctly recite the mission, vision, and process of the church? Could they communicate how their ministry aligns? How are they encouraged to memorize the vision statement?

_____

_____

_____

_____

_____

_____

_____

_____

_____

_____

_____

▶▶SHIFT #5: *From Program to Purpose*

The Why Behind the What—Components of Discipleship

The most common shift churches need is from program to purpose. Leadership has to be willing to measure the outcome of an event or ministry based on how the attendees are growing as disciples of Jesus. Now, if a disciple of Jesus were defined by sitting, attending services in a building, listening, observing, and finally critiquing, then lots of churches would be hitting a home run. But as discussed in week 1, a possible definition of a disciple of Jesus is a person committed to following, being changed by, and on a mission with Jesus. If that is the definition, then how are the ministries in the church doing with making disciples of Jesus? Maybe not so well. This shift from program to purpose is desperately needed.

Each ministry in the church—whether youth, worship, children's, seniors, or even the mountain-biking or bow-hunting ministries—needs to understand that their purpose is to make disciples of Jesus. In other words, anything the church chooses to spend time, energy, and other resources on should clearly be related to making disciples. Can that be said of your church without a major stretching of your definition?

At one point in our church, we found we had said yes to more than fifty ministries. And although all of them would be considered successful at reaching people, we as the leadership had allowed the program to overshadow the purpose. We needed a ministry filter to help us determine whether to say yes or no to a new ministry idea. Here is what we came up with after much prayer and turning to God's Word for direction. Each ministry being proposed had to have the following components, and each leader needed to understand these components (these components should look familiar to you):

MINISTRY FILTER

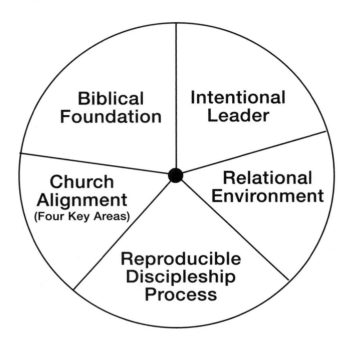

BF + IL + RE + RDP + CA =
Disciple of Jesus Making Disciples of Jesus

So that you can better remember them, here is a brief recap of each one of the five components:

Biblical Foundation
- God desires us to have relationship with Him above all (to love God with all our heart, mind, soul, and strength).
- We need to be involved in deep relationship with others. The second greatest commandment is to love our neighbors as we love ourselves.
- Both Jesus' teachings and methods are valued equally.
- The other four components are being defined through a biblical-foundation lens.

Intentional Leader
- An intentional leader is a person who understands the purpose of the church is to make disciples.
- He or she understands making a disciple of Jesus involves a process of growth.

Relational Environment
- A relational environment is best formed through a group of three to eighteen people, facilitated by a leader who is modeling the fruit of the Spirit (love, joy, peace, patience, and so forth).

- The people involved do life together with a kingdom mindset.
- The relationships go beyond the group time. The individuals move from being strangers to being friends. These relationships press into areas of privacy, transparency, and vulnerability.

Reproducible Discipleship Process

- This method develops people toward Christlikeness and includes three parts: the discipler's part, the disciple's part, and God's part.
- The discipler understands the five stages of spiritual growth, can identify which stage a disciple is in, and knows how to equip each individual at each stage.

Church Alignment (Four Key Areas)

- Relational alignment. A church that is relationally aligned gives relationships the same priority God does. God desires deeply that His creation be reconciled to Him and to each other, be known as lovers of God and others, and be willing to fight for relationship.
- Philosophical alignment. The vision, mission, and process work together to accomplish the purpose of the church.
- Theological alignment. Elders, staff, key volunteers, and key influencers all understand what the church believes and can explain the church's position and beliefs to anyone who asks.
- Organizational alignment. The time in meetings, the dollars being spent, and the energy and focus given inside the church building and outside in the community are very intentionally directed toward keeping the purpose of the church in the forefront.

Day 5

REVIEW AND GROUP DISCUSSION

Pray
Begin your time together in prayer.

Scripture
Choose two volunteers to read Nehemiah 2:1-20 and 8:1-12.

Key Points
- (2:4) Again, Nehemiah was prayerful in forming and communicating a plan.
- (2:5-9) His plan was specific, anticipating needs and obstacles (both people and process).
- (2:11-20) Again, Nehemiah leveraged the power of collective ownership for change. Nehemiah gathered a few chosen men, bringing them along to see for themselves before sharing a plan of action. This built consensus and ownership, allowing others to see the need and develop a desire to lead change.
- (8:1-12) The people rallied together and responded to God's Word.
- (8:1-12) God's Word was (and is) the authority for God's people.
- (8:1-12) It was natural to be upset when recognizing the need for change, but the leaders encouraged the people to rejoice in the faithfulness and strength of God.

Today, our goal is no different than it was in this text. We are seeking to align our lives with the Word of God, making any shifts necessary as individuals and as a community, and recognizing that our identity and strength are based on God's faithfulness. He is still at work. We will not continue to neglect His work.

The Week In Review
Discuss the major points and questions of each day, revisiting anything you may have marked throughout the week for group discussion. Share honestly about where God is challenging and encouraging you. Make sure your group environment is one of mutual respect, tempering observations and responses with grace. Time will not allow you to discuss all the questions, but visit the milestones and make sure each group member has an opportunity to offer input.

Day 1: Biblical foundation and shift #1: from REACHING to MAKING
Day 2: Intentional leadership and shift #2: from INFORMING to EQUIPPING
Day 3: Relational environment and shift #3: from ACTIVITY to RELATIONSHIP
Day 4: Reproducible process and shift #4: from ACCUMULATING to DEPLOYING
        Church alignment and shift #5: from PROGRAM to PURPOSE

Personal "Shifts" As a Disciple

What is God teaching you about Himself? About yourself? About this church?

_____
_____
_____
_____
_____
_____

Week 2 Takeaways

What key truths, principles, or insights will you take away from this week's experience?

_____
_____
_____
_____
_____
_____

Action Steps

What action steps will you prayerfully consider based on this week's experience? Remember, be patient to let God fully develop your action plan. Resist the urge to jump into action immediately. You will revisit these in week 8 to formalize a clear plan of action for leading the DiscipleShift within your context.

_____
_____
_____
_____
_____
_____

Setup for Next Week

Next week will be the final week in our foundational assessments. Our focus has progressively narrowed from general to more specific. A look at biblical baselines and discipleship in general last week moved to shifts within the church. The days leading into our next group discussion will focus on personal areas for leaders within the church. Before we can lead any change in our church and community, we must first honestly prepare our own hearts.

being a leader who makes God proud

Jesus was without question a highly intentional leader. We see in Scripture many of the things He modeled for His disciples and how He regularly debriefed them afterwards. Every step He made created a culture for His disciples, showing them how to lead after He was no longer physically with them. Jesus knew the impact of everything He did and said, where He went, and whom He was with . . . not to mention the impact of what He didn't do and say, where He didn't go, and with whom He chose not to associate.

What about you? Are you aware of the impact of your actions?

This week is gut-check time. Before we can lead any change in our church and community, we must first honestly prepare our own hearts.

Day 1

WHAT IS THE IMPACT OF MY ACTIONS?

Often leaders underestimate the impact they have in the organization. Senior pastors sometimes do not see the weight a simple comment may carry with a staff person, or an elder may not understand why a staff member ran with an idea based on what the elder thought was just a suggestion. Often leaders get excited about an idea and take on a methodology that we sometimes jokingly call "Ready, fire, aim." To lead change in a church, to make key shifts, leaders must have an accurate understanding of the impact of their past, present, and future actions in the church.

Ready . . . Fire . . . Aim!

Describe a time when you did or said something and didn't foresee its negative impact.

_____

_____

_____

_____

_____

_____

Some time ago at RLM we came across a problem that we perceived was due to a lack of clarity on our communication card that went out in our weekly service bulletin. Our senior pastor wanted specific changes to the card, but very little thought was put into the ramifications of the change. (He has given permission for printing this story here; he often shares it himself in training.) He wrote out the changes he wanted, and with some hesitation on the team's part we plowed ahead with what seemed fairly simple. Jim was confident the changes to the card would solve a couple problems we seemed to be having with clarity for people wanting to be baptized. Without any other consideration, investigation, or detail work, I (Luke) moved forward with the idea.

Place a checkmark next to the statement that describes a potential issue that arises when leaders fire before taking time to aim.

_____ The staff has no idea a change was needed.
_____ The volunteers have no idea a change was needed.
_____ The core leadership team may be unclear and uninvested in the senior pastor's idea.
_____ There may be no understanding of how the change may impact multiple other processes in the church.
_____ There may be no clear plan of communication for the whole church.

In our case, all five statements applied. We could have created many more issues, but we hope you can see some of the potential problems that can arise when we try to change without first understanding the impact of those changes. To help effectively lead change, we must begin by investigating that potential impact.

Here is what happened at RLM because of our poor efforts in leading a small change:

- The front office staff became frustrated. They had just printed thousands of cards and would now have to redo the entire printing. The change created more work for them, so they felt we had been inconsiderate.
- The data-entry volunteers had no idea the changes were made, so they did not know to look for the changes on the cards. Thus they overlooked hundreds of requests on the cards, which left people in the church frustrated that they had checked boxes that we never followed up on.
- The staff knew nothing of the changes and were having to deal with frustrated families without knowing where the problem was coming from.
- Those were just a few of the problems. Now, we went back and resolved and ironed out the problem, but this is a small example of how we did not lead well and did not understand the impact and ripple effect of a decision. We fired long before we aimed.

Self-Assessment

Your decisions as a leader have a ripple effect that directly or indirectly impacts three teams. When leading change, you "take aim" by assessing how you impact the leadership rings in your church. Below we have defined those areas with generic team identifiers (names chosen indicate proximity to you, not value or significance):

- **The Immediate Team:** This is your core team and the inner circle that you work with directly. It may include key staff leaders or elders. This is the team of people you are closest to in your job function. This is the central ring of influence.
- **The Larger Team:** These are the people whom the core team directly impacts, the ones who are first to receive communication from the immediate team. They may be staff or volunteers. This is the middle ring of influence.

· **The Outer-Organization Team:** This group is typically made up of volunteers and is the last team to receive communication from the immediate team. They may be the people who are most responsible to carry out the actual change.

The Immediate Team

Write the names of your immediate team.

_____

_____

_____

_____

_____

_____

In the past how have you impacted the individuals on this team? Briefly describe a particular event or circumstance when you worked with this team. Then circle the set of words below that best describe your impact.

_____

_____

_____

_____

_____

Positive and Inquisitive	Directing and Commanding	Unclear and Frustrated
Excited and Hurried	Quiet and Unengaged	Loud and Committed
Angry and Defiant	Supportive and Unclear	Willing and Confident

Look at the set of words you chose and briefly describe how you think that impacted the immediate team.

_____

_____

_____

_____

_____

The Larger Team

Write the names of key people on your larger team, as well as any key ministries that make up this larger team.

_____

_____

_____

_____

_____

_____

Often this group is the first to "feel" the change that is being presented by the immediate team. Sometimes that is good and sometimes not. How would you assess the current relationship between the two teams? Circle the terms that best describe that relationship:

Positive and Supportive   Uneasy and Speculative   Hurt and Wounded
Confident and Optimistic   New and Unknown   Disconnected and Confused

Why did you choose those words? What role have you played in creating the current environment?

_____

_____

_____

_____

_____

The Outer-Organization Team

To get a more complete understanding of your impact as you lead change, you must evaluate your outer team. Leaders often make the mistake of not evaluating how they have impacted the outer layers of leadership in the church. To help you avoid that mistake, begin your evaluation by identifying the specific people and ministries that make up this team.

Assess the relationship the Immediate Team and the Larger Team have with the Outer-Organizational Team. Again, circle the terms that best describe the relationship:

Positive and Supportive   Uneasy and Speculative   Hurt and Wounded
Confident and Optimistic   New and Unknown   Disconnected and Confused

Why did you circle those particular terms? What role you have played in creating the current environment?

_____

_____

_____

_____

_____

Finally, consider the impact of your actions, not just your decisions and communication, on the people around you. It is one thing to say something; it may be an entirely different thing to model it. Modeling is a vital part of the leadership and discipleship relationships.

What are some examples of Jesus "practicing what He preached," or simply leading by example, letting His action speak for itself?

_____

_____

_____

_____

_____

_____

How are you modeling discipleship to your team so they want to follow you? What are you are modeling that helps your team follow your lead?

_____

_____

_____

_____

_____

_____

_____

_____

In what ways are you not modeling discipleship to your team? Do you still expect them to follow or obey the direction? What are you modeling that may make it challenging for your team to follow you?

_____

_____

_____

_____

_____

_____

In what ways might something you've been frustrated about be pointing to a behavior that is being modeled?

_____

_____

_____

_____

_____

_____

BEING A COURAGEOUS LEADER

Day 2

Being a courageous leader takes different forms based on the situation you are facing. On day 1 you were reminded that as a leader your words and actions impact the people and environments around you both positively and negatively. The question is are you willing to discover that impact?

The writer of the book of Proverbs declared in the opening verses that his purpose was to gain "wisdom" and "insight" and warned that "fools despise wisdom and instruction" (see Proverbs 1:2-7). As leaders, we must constantly seek insight and wisdom—not just related to our fields of expertise, but also in regard to ourselves as leaders.

The Johari window is a simple and useful tool for illustrating and improving self-awareness and mutual understanding between individuals within a group. The Johari window has four regions or windows:

1. **Open area:** what is known by the person about him- or herself and is also known by others
2. **Blind area (or blind spot):** what is unknown by the person about him- or herself but that others know
3. **Hidden area:** what the person knows about him- or herself that others do not know
4. **Unknown area (or unknown self):** what is unknown by the person about him- or herself and is also unknown by others

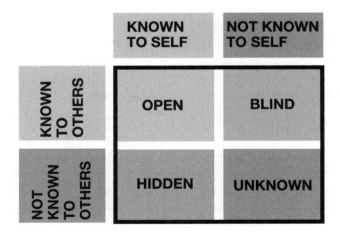

Today we will look at two of these areas: the "open" area and the "blind" area. First we'll investigate your blinds spots as a leader and the impact those blinds spots are having on your team and your environment.

Have you thought much about the kind of environment you have created (healthy or unhealthy)? Do you want a healthy environment? Healthy meaning "Christlike," where people are drawn in and want to be part of what is happening. The environment is loving, caring, joyful, peaceful, directed, gentle, and grace-giving. In a healthy environment mistakes are accepted and feedback is desired. You get the idea.

Oftentimes leaders are not aware of how their actions are creating and developing the environment around them. Whether positive or negative, you are creating an environment. The question is are you aware of what you are creating? Are there some elements of the environment that are propelling your team forward? What are they? Likewise, are there parts of the environment that are holding your team back from being all that Christ created them to be?

_____

_____

_____

_____

_____

_____

_____

Self-Awareness, Self-Assessment

Before we dive into our environment and what we have created, we need to start with ourselves and what is known to us and others, the open area of the Johari window.

If you asked people around you to describe your leadership with seven words (five positive and two negative), what do you think those words would be?

Positive _____

_____

Negative _____

_____

For each trait answer the following: When I am leading and interacting with people, I at times can be described as _____,

The impact of my being this way on others (spouse, family, team, staff) is _____

_____

_____

_____

_____

_____

_____

These attributes (5) positively and (2) negatively impact the people around you. Is that difficult for you to accept? Why?

_____

_____

_____

_____

_____

_____

_____

Look again at the two negative traits. You may notice that what you have identified as a negative is just a strength being overdone. Did you catch that? Your negative trait is probably a strength being overdone. For example, you might have described yourself negatively as aggressive. However, aggressiveness stated positively could be called determination. You want to accomplish great things, get the job done, but maybe you need to dial it down a notch or two.

Great job at looking into the open or known part of the Johari window. Now let's dive into the blind area. To accomplish this we are going to need some data that is known to others about your leadership but is not known to you. For this exercise, you'll need to collect responses from three to five people you are close to relationally. You'll ask them three questions, but first you'll help them understand why you want to know the answers.

Be open to the possibility that the people you ask may feel a little uncomfortable based on your past interactions. Also it will be important that you validate what you heard them say in response to your questions. Oftentimes the listener does not accurately hear what the other person is saying and therefore receives inaccurate data. So please make sure you validate the responses and say thank you after each answered question. Saying thank you will go a long way toward letting them know you really do have a genuine desire to know how you have been impacting people around you.

Helping someone understand the "why" behind the questions could look like this:

"Bill, do you have minute? I'd like to ask you something personal about myself."

"Sure," says Bill. "I have a few minutes."

"Excellent. I'm completing a workbook that asks a lot of questions and is helping me to reflect on a variety of areas. This week's topic is self-awareness and the impact my words and actions may be having on my fellow team members and others around me, both positive and negative. I was wondering if you would be willing—being as honest as you feel safe enough to be—to answer three questions about me."

Bill hesitates but says, "Sure."

You notice the hesitation and reassure him you want the feedback and that he will be helping you see into your "blinds spots."

"Okay," Bill says. "What's the first question?"

"Thanks," you say. "I appreciate your willingness to help. Oh, and one more thing. I would like to validate what I hear you saying after you answer each question, and I need you to let me know if I've captured what you said accurately. Does that work for you?"

There you have it. It's not a difficult process, but it may not be easy.

The next step is for you to select your people to interview. Write their names below.

1. _____

2. _____

3. _____

4. _____

5. _____

Here are the three questions. Make sure you record their answers while you're together. You can transfer them to the lines below later.

1. What do you see about "me being me" that impacts people in a positive way?

_____

_____

_____

_____

_____

_____

2. What do you see about my words or actions that may be causing some unnecessary tensions or possibly unwanted feelings?

_____

_____

_____

_____

_____

_____

_____

3. What five words would you use to describe me?

_____

_____

_____

_____

_____

_____

Summarize the responses to describe how you are impacting the people around you in a positive way.

_____

_____

_____

_____

_____

_____

What recurring themes or consistent answers do you see in the responses to question 1?

_____
_____
_____
_____
_____

What recurring themes or consistent answers do you see in the responses to question 2?

_____
_____
_____
_____
_____

What recurring themes or consistent answers do you see in the responses to question 3?

_____
_____
_____
_____
_____

Impact on the Environment

Based on the feedback you received to question 1, what kind environment are you creating?

_____
_____
_____
_____
_____

Based on the feedback you received to question 2, what kind environment are you creating?

_____
_____
_____
_____
_____

Based on the feedback you received to question 3, what kind environment are you creating?

_____

_____

_____

_____

_____

_____

_____

Now that you've experienced receiving feedback, you'll have an opportunity to provide it for your group members. Fill in the chart below with the names of your group members and five traits you think best describe them. (Be prepared to share one word for each person during the group time.)

Name	Trait	Trait	Trait	Trait	Trait

One of the purposes of this exercise it to help you intentionally look at how your teammates are uniquely crafted by God and how those qualities impact the people and the environment around you.

WHAT DO YOU SEE?

Day 3

John pastored a 100-year-old church that was made up of about 150 people. God was working in John's heart to show him that something needed to change. The church had not seen a new convert in the four years he had been pastoring there. No one felt a need to invite their friends, and the church was stuck in a deep rut with no motivation to get out. The ministries were extremely programmatic and felt more like little clubs than anything that was reaching out to the dying world. Anytime a visitor did come to the church, John was embarrassed by the "churchy" feel and the cold shoulder that seemed to be given by the congregation.

The Lord lit a fire in John. He began to share in his sermons how God was working in his heart, and the Lord led him to read some of our materials. John and three other men in the church began meeting to pray. They opened up and began to do life together. From that time, a revolution in the hearts of the people began.

Seeing The Gaps

1. Below is a list of environmental truths about the church John was leading. Write the letter in the blank that connect those truths to the scripture that contradicts what they were doing.

1. _____ No one saw a need to share their faith.   a. Ephesians 4:12-14
2. _____ The ministries were isolated programs.   b. Galatians 5:13-15
3. _____ The environment was not friendly.   c. 1 Corinthians 12:15-20
4. _____ No one was being raised up to make disciples.   d. Romans 10:10-17
(1-d, 2-b, 3-b, 4-a)

John told us he continued to see more instances in which the energy in the church was going in multiple (and often wrong) directions, and opportunities for service were being lost. Jesus even addressed this issue within the Jewish culture of the leaders leading people in the wrong direction. They had lost their focus and were pursuing the wrong things.

Opportunity Cost

In order for you and the leadership team to effectively shift the culture of your church to one of vibrant spiritual life and growth, you must identify the areas that are costing you. Where are you expending effort that at the end of the day does not translate into disciples made?

1. List the ministries or projects in your church that do not result in disciples made (or it is a far stretch to say that they do).

_____

_____

_____

_____

_____

2. Make your best estimate of the percentage of your actual financial and energy commitment goes to those ministries or programs.

_____ % of financial budget   _____ % of church energy

For you as a leader to understand how many of your resources are being directed at what does not produce a win is key. Knowing that information helps you reveal the gaps in accomplishing what God has called you to do. It helps you to create necessary and beneficial tension within the church if they can see the actual problem. This in turn helps you cast vision.

Giving Vision

Vision is a word the church loves to throw around. In fact the word has been seriously overused. In this case, though, casting a vision is truly what needs to be done. At the beginning of today's lesson we told you about John and his church. What helped John move his church body was showing his church the gaps they had, as well as the opportunity cost by doing so many other things that took away from effectively making disciples.

Now, not everyone in the body was okay with this initially. People were very attached to their ministries, and some did not want anything to change. Church attendance even went down over the next six months, but the wheels of change were being put in motion and the church was on its way to a much healthier and productive future. (These are practical points we will explore in upcoming chapters.)

3. What are your fears regarding showing your church body the gaps that exist in where you are and where you know the church should be? (Be prepared to share your answer with your group.)

_____
_____
_____
_____
_____
_____
_____

4. What are your fears regarding cutting or changing the ministries or projects that are creating opportunity costs in your church? (Be prepared to share your answer with your group.)

_____
_____
_____
_____
_____
_____
_____
_____

Finally, today we are going to look at how to accurately align ministries, how to put all of your energy behind a unified direction. This is a simple but possibly radical change of course necessary in making the *DiscipleShift*.

The tool we use is called the 2x2 ministry matrix. The matrix asks important questions that enable the leadership to walk away with several small aligning changes to shift the ministry toward the direction of change. It looks like this:

MINISTRY MATRIX

PASSION

Hobby · Life's Mission

PROFIT 0 — 10 **PROFIT**

Waste of Time · Busy Work

PASSION

Profit

Profit is the change you are trying to lead toward. Your profit is your clear win. At Real Life Ministries we have also included discipleship or spiritual maturity under profit. So, then, using the 2x2 ministry matrix we would evaluate a ministry on the natural outcome of profit. The less likely the ministry is to challenge people to actually grow in Christ the farther to the left we would mark the X-axis or profit. For example, the men's basketball ministry would be closer to the left than a men's Bible study. Now, you may decide that you define profit differently in your organization, but the same rules apply regardless.

Passion

The Y-axis is passion, or how much energy can be generated with this particular ministry. Using the men's basketball ministry as an example again, the passion there might be sky high. Men of all ages can't wait until the season starts. You can barely announce it before all the teams are filled. You don't have to work very hard to get people excited about a ministry if it is high on the passion scale. Likewise, the lower the passion, the farther to the right on the Y-axis it will be evaluated. As you might guess, men's basketball was evaluated to be high on the Y-axis because of the high level of passion. However, it was also evaluated to be low in profit, so it was low on the X-axis.

To discover a ministry's outcome, you simply align the X and Y axes, using the four possible outcomes of evaluating a ministry on the 2x2 ministry matrix.

Waste of Time
(Bottom Left = Low Profit + Low Passion)

If a ministry is considered to be a waste of time, it has been evaluated to be low on both profit and passion. The result would be to eliminate the ministry altogether. We have had to do that with several ministries and events that were worth trying but just not worth repeating.

Busy Work
(Bottom Right = High Profit + Low Passion)

When a ministry or event on your schedule is of very little or low passion but has a minimal amount of profit it is classified as busy work. For instance, I (Luke) hate looking at budgets; I have a very low passion for financial matters. However, I also know that if I don't pay attention to my budget, my chances of discipling with new people will be hurt. Therefore, budget does have some profit attached to it, so budgets are in the category of busy work. Busy work is very difficult to make more of a success by modifying the activity. With such a low passion rating, those tasks will always be just busy work and (unfortunately) still worth doing.

Hobby
(Top Left = Low Profit + High Passion)

As in the example of the men's basketball ministry, a hobby has a higher amount of passion but a lower level of profit. The solution is not to cut it, but to look at the possibility of modifying the ministry to make it more profitable. We will go over this later.

Life's Mission
(Top Right = High Profit + High Passion)

We put activities in this category in the rare event that a ministry is high in both passion and profit. For example, home groups or small groups—where all of the people are excited to meet together and are able to mature in Christ through a relational environment—fit in the life's mission quadrant. Leading a growing group like that brings a great sense of fulfillment. Even better, when you're discipling a couple that matures to the point of leading their own group with new people, the activity falls under life's mission. This category is the win we are trying to achieve in a church. It is why the congregation wakes up in the morning. It is the reason your church exists, and it gives the entire organization hope and energy to grow.

Enter some of your ministries or past events on the 2x2 ministry matrix. What did you discover about those events or ministries?

_____

_____

_____

_____

_____

_____

MINISTRY MATRIX

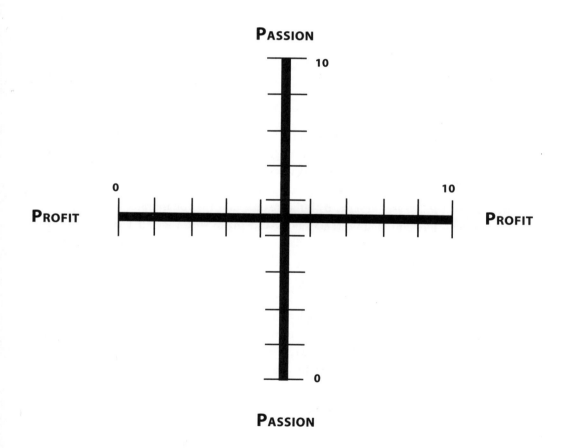

Day 4

WHERE IS GOD CALLING YOU TO LEAD?

Consider your own passion and profit. Are you personally aligned to best advance the purpose of the church? Maybe you have been asked, "What wakes you up in the morning?" In other words, what are you personally passionate about? Most of us would like to respond with "Christ's church" or "the kingdom" or "the gospel." But if you really want to know what your value system is perceived to be, ask your children, "What am I passionate about?" The answer they give is what you are consistently communicating to them through your actions, emotions, and verbiage to be most important.

Passion

Ask your children and/or people who know you the best, "What am I passionate about?" Write their responses below.

_____

_____

_____

_____

_____

Many of us are guilty of sending mixed messages with our church, small groups, or ministries. As leadership at RLM we decided to go into great detail about what a win looks like for each of those areas. We have boiled a win down to our "7 Essentials," which are (1) abide in Christ; (2) reach the lost; (3) connect the unconnected; (4) chase the strays; (5) identify, equip, release leaders; (6) build teams; and (7) collaborate. RLM's goal was to communicate previously unspoken values and make sure that all facets of ministry aligned with producing these seven essentials. Making this change in communication has brought clarity and energy to the entire church.

Many churches now have goals, catchy sayings, or a Scripture verse that represents the aligning win for the entire organization. For a particular small group, maybe the win is the reason or goal for meeting. If you are leading a ministry, your aligning win is the main thing that the entire team is focused on and working together to accomplish. You, as the leader, should be talking about the win, the main thing, and the reason you exist. Your teams need to have absolute clarity on this issue.

In your ministry environment ask the group, "What is a win for this church (or group or ministry)?" Record their responses below.

_____

_____

_____

_____

_____

Communicating the win for everyone is an important and critical piece of leadership. We can't be truly unified if we don't know what the goal or win is. We can love each other and be Christians, but without agreeing to our goals we are just friends, not co-laborers. On a scale of 1 to 10—1 being disunity and 10 being complete unity on the organizational clarity of "what is a win"—where do you see your church or organization? Put an X on the line to indicate where you feel you are on the scale.

1_____10

Now that you see a bit better the importance of being unified and having focus, you may be wondering how to move your church or organization closer to a 10. The good news is that you are already doing the most important thing. You are communicating what the win is for the team you are leading. The more you communicate the win, the more the group will start to migrate toward a 10. The real discovery from today should be that everyone has something he or she is passionate about. Sometimes that passion can communicate mixed messages to what a win truly is for you and the church. Hopefully, the more you communicate the definition of a win, the more people will join the effort with their different gifts, abilities, and passions.

Alignment and unity within any organization is paramount, especially one that professes to be following Christ. Read the following verses regarding alignment and unity:

How good and pleasant it is when God's people live together in unity! (Psalm 133:1)

My prayer is not for them alone. I pray also for those who will believe in me through their message, that all of them may be one, Father, just as you are in me and I am in you. May they also be in us so that the world may believe that you have sent me. I have given them the glory that you gave me, that they may be one as we are one—I in them and you in me—so that they may be brought to complete unity. Then the world will know that you sent me and have loved them even as you have loved me. (John 17:20-23)

Just as a body, though one, has many parts, but all its many parts form one body, so it is with Christ. For we were all baptized by one Spirit so as to form one body—whether Jews or Gentiles, slave or free—and we were all given the one Spirit to drink. Even so the body is not made up of one part but of many. (1 Corinthians 12:12-14)

As a prisoner for the Lord, then, I urge you to live a life worthy of the calling you have received. Be completely humble and gentle; be patient, bearing with one another in love. Make every effort to keep the unity of the Spirit through the bond of peace. There is one body and one Spirit, just as you were called to one hope when you were called; one Lord, one faith, one baptism; one God and Father of all, who is over all and through all and in all. (Ephesians 4:1-6)

Alignment

Yesterday you did some critical, and maybe uncomfortable, exercises using the 2x2 ministry matrix. This helpful tool assisted you in determining how to best unify the efforts of the church around its purpose and mission. As a leader, it is essential for you to communicate the vision God has given so the church can rally together. A body must be unified in its efforts and direction. When the church is unified, Christ can be glorified. When we all work toward the same goal, we can accomplish far more than we can when we work very hard but in different directions. So today we take another step toward putting all the pieces together that we've been looking at over the past several weeks.

Based on your definitions of a disciple (from week 1 day 3), what is your vision?

If our goal as Christians is to make disciples, then what does winning look like for your church? (Be prepared to share your answer with your group.)

Finally, what do you believe God may be leading you to do within your ministry/circle of influence to bring alignment to your church according to the above definitions?

REVIEW AND GROUP DISCUSSION

Day 5

Pray

Begin your time together in prayer.

Scripture

Today we will jump to the end of the story of Nehemiah. Leadership is about vision and knowing where you want to be at the end of our own story.

Choose three people to read Nehemiah 13:14, 22, 30-31.

Key Points

+ While the actions taken were extreme, Nehemiah was passionate about the people of God living by the Word of God.
+ Nehemiah knew the difference he wanted to make with his life and leadership.
+ Three times in this chapter he repeated this sentiment: "Remember me for this, my God, and show mercy to me according to your great love." The last words of the entire book are "Remember me with favor, my God."
How will our lives be remembered by God and by His people?

The Week In Review

Discuss the major points and questions of each day, revisiting anything you may have marked throughout the week for group discussion. Share honestly about where God is challenging and encouraging you. Make sure your group environment is one of mutual respect, tempering observations and responses with grace. Time will not allow you to discuss all the questions, but visit the milestones and make sure each group member has an opportunity to offer input.

Day 1: What is the impact of my actions?
Day 2: Being a courageous leader
Day 3: What do you see?
Day 4: Where is God calling you to lead?

Personal "Shifts" As a Disciple

What is God teaching you about Him? About yourself? About this church?

_____

_____

_____

_____

_____

_____

_____

Week 3 Takeaways

What key truths, principles, and/or insights will you take away from this week's experience?

_____

_____

_____

_____

_____

_____

Action Steps

What action steps will you prayerfully consider based on this week's experience? Remember, be patient to let God fully develop your action plan. Resist the urge to jump into action immediately. You will revisit these in week 8 to formalize a clear plan of action for leading the DiscipleShift within your context.

_____

_____

_____

_____

_____

_____

_____

Setup For Next Week

As leaders who desire to make God proud, how do we begin to shift our energy and efforts toward becoming a disciple-making church? Next week we will begin breaking down the practical steps of leading change, specifically leading the DiscipleShift.

healthy tension and building support

So often in the church, leaders and church members do not see a need for change. Even when change is presented, the common response is "we have never done it that way before." People resist change! As a leadership team you have to create tension between the current situation and the need to move forward. People must feel a sense of urgency to change whatever is not correct or effective ministry within the kingdom. In *Leading Change,* author John Kotter talks about this issue in the context of the corporate world. He makes a very transferable point for the church when he says, "Establishing a sense of urgency is crucial to gaining needed cooperation. With complacency high, transformations usually go nowhere because few people are even interested in working on changing the problem" (John P. Kotter, *Leading Change* [Boston: Harvard Business School Press, 1996], p. 36).

Day 1

THE POWER OF INVITATION

Have you ever heard the saying "You've got to go with the goers"? When making a shift and building the necessary tension in your organization, you have to begin to look for those who will join you first. These are the staff and/or key volunteers who have already bought in to creating biblical disciples in relational environments. These people will be an invaluable resource to help create momentum.

Several years ago at RLM, we believed God was leading us to make some significant change to help us be more effective in biblical disciple-making. Up to that point, we had grown so fast that we had not structured our small-group ministries to handle the massive growth. To continue to live out our mission of making disciples we needed to make major changes. Doing so, we knew, would impact hundreds of relationships.

After much planning and prayer, our leadership team began to reach out to include some of the key volunteers who would help champion the change. These key volunteers were brought in, vision was cast for them and they were given the opportunity to provide input to some of the details to carry out this radical change in our church.

Where Do We Start?

1. Before looking at who you will bring onboard, it is important to take a close look at which ministries in your church have the most influence. List the ministries in your church, starting with the one you believe has the highest level of influence.

_____   _____
_____   _____
_____   _____
_____   _____
_____   _____
_____   _____

Most leaders do not do this exercise and just assume people will follow their lead once they cast what they believe to be a compelling vision. Sometimes the most influential ministries are small in personnel or budget, but are very influential due to the leader or service they provide. To overlook this step and not evaluate your ministries can be catastrophic to change.

2. Why might it be a mistake to not evaluate influential ministries in your church?

_____
_____
_____
_____
_____
_____
_____

Us-Versus-Them Mentality

If your leadership team does not reach out, invite people in, and take into consideration influential ministries, you will create a strong opposition that does not have to be. We call it the "us-versus-them mentality." This is when a separation is felt between two groups in the church. One group feels like they are left out or change is being done to them rather than with them. This mentality can also occur when the organization has done a poor job of leading change up to this point. People never felt part of the change or even felt totally left out. There may not be any way to correct what was done, but to ignore it can be damaging.

3. Read the statements below and place an X next to those that would indicate that a group of people in your church have a strong us-versus-them mentality.

   a. _____ I can't believe they are changing the ministry this way! What are they thinking?
   b. _____ I have served in this ministry for six years, and I had no idea we were not going to do this event anymore!
   c. _____ We heard a rumor that the vision of our church is changing. When was the leadership going to include us small group leaders in this decision?

In all three statements above you can see an us-versus-them in the language. The "speakers" in those statements clearly felt excluded from the decision to change, as well as surprised and dismayed by the actions of leadership.

4. When was change led poorly in your church? How can you show consideration to those who may be hurt by or unsure of change? (Be prepared to share your answers with your group.)

_____
_____
_____
_____
_____
_____
_____

Going after and inviting people to be involved is one of the most exciting and important parts of building a team to lead change. Begin to pray now about whom God would have you include in this group.

5. Fill out the chart below by creating a list of key individuals you believe could help champion change in your church. Write their first names and the ministries they are involved in. Then, in the third column rate the person from 1 to 5 on level of influence (1 being low overall organizational influence and 5 being very high).

Name	Ministry Involved	Influence

We not only have to invite people to be a part of the change. We have to actually empower them to be part of the change. Again we found a key transferable point from Kotter's book on leading change: "Environmental change demands organizational change. Major internal transformation rarely happens unless many people assist" (Kotter, 101–102). Often leaders underestimate the involvement of volunteers in the church, so, as we mentioned, when change happens the volunteers may feel like it is being done to them rather than done with them.

6. Think about a time when you were part of an organizational change. How were you included in that process? How well did it go?

_____

_____

_____

_____

_____

A Win Story

When we were leading through a small-group ministry structure change, I (Brandon) knew the input of our volunteers was key. Our staff was onboard, but many of the key volunteers had no idea what we were thinking. So I reserved an offsite location and invited many of our key small-group volunteers to an overnight retreat. In our first session Jim Putman and I presented the vision of where God was leading and how we were stuck structurally. We put the problem back on the volunteers and asked for their input. For the next day and a half the volunteers came up with practical ideas that helped us overcome some of our struggles. In that process they took ownership of the problem and led significant change in our church. It was a special time in our church history.

7. How could you gather your volunteer leaders to cast vision and invite them to be a part of the change? (Be prepared to share your answers with your group.)

_____

_____

_____

_____

_____

Review:

- Know the ministries that have the most influence.
- Invite people to be a part of the change.
- Work hard to avoid creating an us-versus-them mentality.

You Can't Do It Alone

On May 25, 1961, to jumpstart the United States back into competing with the Soviet Union in a "space race," then President John F. Kennedy delivered a speech titled "Special Message to the Congress on Urgent National Needs." He stated that the United States should set as a goal "landing a man on the moon and returning him safely to the earth" by the end of the decade. As you know, that challenge from leadership became a reality on July 16, 1969. In reality, a massive effort of human achievement was already underway when the president delivered his speech. Before he made his bold statement to Congress, Kennedy had consulted with many trusted people who promised to deliver results.

Leading healthy change requires a team of people. One person leading healthy change alone is not only improbable but impossible. There are several reasons why one person can't lead change by him- or herself. First, one person never will be able to get complete and accurate information on the environment. Because no issue is flat or single-sided, one person's perspective on the problem and the solutions is simply not adequate. To understand a challenge from multiple angles requires many sets of trusted eyes and ears—a team. Another reason we need a team to lead healthy change in an organization is because a team brings diversity. We all have individual strengths and weaknesses, gifts and abilities. One person acting alone does not have all the gifts, tools, and experience that an entire team of people has. Finally, the most important reason of all: it's biblical. First Corinthians 12:27 says, "Now you are the body of Christ, and each one of you is a part of it." We are supposed to work together to form a team, the body of Christ. When we are unified, God is glorified.

Perspective, wider range of skills, and biblical alignment are all reasons to work with a team rather than leading change on your own. What are some other reasons?

_____

_____

_____

_____

_____

The rest of this week we are going to cover how to build a team that can lead change. A good starting point is to understand the requirements for team members. People on the team need to have the abilities and leadership roles that enable them to make decisions that can be translated into action. If this team doesn't have the ability or the positioning, then it will be a huge waste of time and a source of great frustration. The team will work hard and may even come up with some good ideas to lead change throughout the church. However, the team won't be recognized by other leaders of the church who weren't already part of the change discussion, and it will be quickly and quietly dismissed.

Which individuals have positions of authority that would qualify them to be considered for this team?

_____

_____

_____

_____

_____

_____

With the help of your group, narrow the list down to names you all agree on. Then consider which skills, abilities, or experience you might be missing from the team.

_____

_____

_____

_____

_____

_____

Which individuals in your church may not have the necessary authority but do have the abilities lacking from your first list?

_____

_____

_____

_____

_____

_____

This team will not only be able to make healthy change in the church. It can become a model for what the church is supposed to look like. The team itself will start to become a relational environment. How better to lead change than showing the rest of the church.

How can a church grow and be attractive to unbelievers who are desperate for healthy relationship when the church can't give any examples of what a communal relationship looks like? Community must be at the heart of the church. Unbelievers will only be attracted by fancy buildings and well-executed performances onstage for a period of time. The love they experience through a communal church is life-changing because only through a community can they experience satisfying relationships with God and others.

Day 2

CREATING CHEMISTRY

While no team is perfect, you can assemble a great team that God has uniquely gifted to carry out a fresh vision. Yesterday you identified influential people in your church with essential skills and abilities. Today we are going to dig in to how you can quickly build this dream team into a cohesive unit. This is the team that has been selected for leading change at your church—leading the *DiscipleShift*.

Basic Chemistry 101

The first three phases of building the team are intended to be completed in one meeting. It may seem like a lot to cover, but each of the first three phases is intended to build upon the previous one. Therefore, the first three phases must be worked through in one gathering.

PHASE 1: ORIENTATION

The first step in team building is called the "orientation phase." Even though many of the people might already know why they have been called to your first meeting individually, they need to hear you say it to the group. The team needs to be treated as a unit and therefore communicated to as a unit, so you'll need to address why this team has been assembled.

The need of the people on the team to hear the reason they have been called together is huge. Each person, regardless of position or ability, is wondering about their potential fit on the team and whether the other people selected will accept them. Clarity encourages confidence and ownership. If you don't satisfy their need to know why they were called into this room as a group, they will remain guarded, uncertain, uncommitted, or even fearful.

Going over the purpose of why you are gathering as a team may seem redundant and a waste of time. You might feel the pull to move on to implementation now. Here is a warning: If you skip one of these phases and don't lead through it correctly, the team will not gel and you will have to go back. Each one of these phases must be presented to the team if you want the group to be high functioning.

The orientation phase, simply put, is the need for each individual to understand why they have been selected. If they respond with the pride of membership, move on to the next phase. If any member of the team responds in fear and uncertainty, then restate why they are assembled.

How are you going to communicate to the team why they have all been called? Specifically identify strengths and the purpose each member was chosen for this team. (Be prepared to share your answers with the group.)

PHASE 2: TRUST-BUILDING

The next phase is called the "trust-building phase." Don't worry; no one on the team is going to have to get on a table, fall backward, and hope the team catches them. This phase is simply "who are you?" Each person on this dream team wants to know why the other members have been called. What are the agendas and competencies of each member of the team?

It is vital for people to talk about themselves so the team can hear that person's heart. You have already identified why you have chosen each person from an organizational standpoint. The team now wants to know about who each person is at a relational level—even if you know for a fact that every person in the room has known the others for years. This step in building a team cannot be skipped in rallying excitement and ownership from a group that is carrying out a vision, not merely a task.

Two great questions for this phase are "What does this church mean to you and your family?" and "What wakes you up in the morning, or how has God wired you to give Him glory?" Just those two questions answered by team members can make a huge impact and prepare the group to move to the next phase of building the team.

Try it for yourself! Take a few moments to answer both of the questions. (Be prepared to share your answers with your group.)

What does this church mean to you and your family?

_____

_____

_____

_____

_____

_____

_____

What wakes you up in the morning, or how has God wired you to give Him glory?

_____

_____

_____

_____

_____

_____

This phase is so important. Sharing builds trust and a free exchange among team members because they respect each other. When you see each team member able to speak the truth and observe the other members respond with mutual regard for each other, you have completed the trust-building phase. If you feel the entire group not letting their guards down and putting up a "professional/church face," then repeat this phase with other questions and/or activities. You may need to get people out of an office/meeting environment for success in this phase.

What high-functioning teams have you been on? What was the level of trust among members on that team?

_____
_____
_____
_____
_____
_____
_____
_____

PHASE 3: GOAL-CLARIFICATION

Now we are ready for the third phase of building the dream team—the "goal-clarification phase." In this important phase the team will learn what they will do as a team. The leader of the team should be ready for discussing team goals and striving to gain clarity through vision. This is the "I have called you all together today for this reason" part of the meeting. The dream team needs to know what they are trying to accomplish in order to move to the next step.

We caution you to give your team the goal without a lot of other parameters. Giving the team too many details for the purpose of structure will only hamstring them as they try to fit into your box. If this team starts to function highly effectively, they will undoubtedly outperform even your expectations.

If the team understands the goal of what they are to accomplish as a unit, they will naturally respond. The team will begin to make explicit assumptions about what to do next with a shared vision. They will start to move as a team with automatic clarity and integrated goals. If the first two phases are completed, then in this third phase—the goal-clarification phase—the team will start to take on a life of its own.

If the team is still confused about what their goals are for succeeding, then they will respond in apathy, skepticism, and irrelevant competition. If this occurs, you will have to start this phase again.

Write down exactly what you will say to launch the goal-clarification phase toward success.

_____
_____
_____
_____
_____
_____
_____

Advanced Chemistry

With these three phases now behind you, the team will work as a unit and begin to move faster than the leader can lead. From here on, the team will move so quickly and naturally together that it will feel almost automatic. We will go over the following phases only to make sure the team is still where it should be and not starting to get off-track.

PHASE 4: COMMITMENT

In the next phase, the "commitment phase," the team starts to makes decisions about how they are going to accomplish the goal. If the team is tracking properly, members should start automatically assigning roles, allocating resources, and making decisions. The leadership that formed the team might want to take control as the team starts to pick up more and more momentum, but that would be a mistake! Let the team function as a team and slingshot themselves into the next phase of building the team. If the team is getting off-track and not able to move through this phase, the members will start to respond with dependence and resistance.

How will you safeguard yourself and other leaders from interfering in the dream team's sudden momentum?

_____

_____

_____

_____

_____

_____

_____

_____

PHASE 5: IMPLEMENTATION

In the next phase, called the "implementation phase," the team starts adding details to their collective decisions made in the previous phase. The team will automatically decide who does what, when, and where. The team will work more seamlessly and intuitively as what they learned about each other in phase 2 comes into practice as they assign roles for the future. If the team is still tracking, they should be automatically forming clear processes, alignment, and disciplined execution.

Have you ever been part of a team or organization that performs at this level? What was your experience? (Be prepared to share your answers with the group.)

_____

_____

_____

_____

_____

_____

If this phase is causing the team to veer off course, the team will respond in conflict and confusion, nonalignment and missed deadlines. This is where your preparation will really start to pay off, because you created a team that is balanced between big-picture thinkers and detail-oriented members. If the team were full of only big-picture thinkers it would stall. However, if the team didn't have enough of those big-picture people who are capable of creating ideas and dreams, the team would probably not have made it to this phase at all.

PHASE 6: HIGH-PERFORMANCE

The last phase is called the "high-performance phase." This is where the team starts to execute their plan, making necessary changes while staying aligned with each other. If the team is still on track during this phase you will witness spontaneous interaction, synergy, and expectation-surpassing results. If the team is starting to get off-track, then you will notice overload and disharmony.

This team will have accomplished so much for the church and leading healthy change. How are you going to celebrate with them? How will you honor them and still direct glory to God?

PAINTING THE TENSION

Day 3

Creating change in any church body can be like trying to extract an abscessed tooth from an angry lion—nearly an impossible task. As an individual and a group, the next steps will possibly push you over the top. You will move past the theoretical to the actual steps to incorporate change. We are going to help you kindly, lovingly, yet firmly and confidently, jerk that abscessed tooth out of that lion's head—in the name of Jesus, of course. To do this you must help the lion to feel better, to understand that the tooth has got to come out!

Church Awareness

At this point you are just over halfway through the workbook and you have gained insight into your personal and team leadership as well as begun to get clarity on your corporate vision and communication. The next step is to evaluate and look at how to bring awareness to the church. As a leadership team, you must begin to discuss how to "paint the tension" for your people. Painting the tension means to begin to give them a picture of where the church needs to go and how off course you currently are.

1. Place an X on the line that demonstrates where you think your church body is in its recognition of the change that needs to happen.

●————————————————————————————————————●

in the dark   slight glimmer   seeing the light   embracing the light

Jesus faced the same problem. He had groups of people all around Him that would have been at varying places on the line above. Those people (including the disciples) had no idea how far off-course they were. Jesus painted the tension in several ways to show what the people currently believed and how far they were from the heart of God.

1. Draw a line that connects Jesus's method of painting the tension among the people to the Scripture passage that describes it.

1. Stories and parables	A. Matthew 8:5-13
2. Others living it out	B. John 10:1-21
3. Modeling with His own life	C. Mark 4:1-20
4. Preaching to the crowds	D. John 8:1-11

You should have connected the following 1 to C, 2 to A, 3 to D, and 4 to B.

Telling Stories And Parables

Stories and parables are a key method Jesus used to teach biblical truth and to begin to change people's perspectives on a variety of topics. This method brought tension and helped create change. For your leadership team we suggest using the same powerful method. In our church we use stories of what God is doing in several areas.

Below is a list of areas where you may consider using stories or testimonies to help people see that the church is off-course. This can help create tension for change.

> Testimonial video during services
> Article in a church newsletter
> Church website
> Weekly service announcements

1. In what specific ways could you use stories and parables to help the church feel the tension of being off-course?

_____

_____

_____

_____

_____

_____

Others Living It Out

At RLM, one of the best ways to lead through change was to give examples of people within our church who were living out the change we wanted. This is different than just telling a story or giving a parable. We put the actual story right in front of our church. This helps people see what the church leadership believes in and how it aligns with biblical truth. A wonderful biblical picture of this is found in the verses you read earlier in Matthew 8 about the Roman centurion.

2. When have you seen somebody living out biblical truth? What impact did it have on you?

_____

_____

_____

_____

_____

3. How could your leadership team put testimonies of others living out the change you want to see in front of your church? (Be prepared to share your answer with your group.)

_____

_____

_____

_____

_____

_____

Modeling It with His Own Life

In the first four weeks of the workbook, we talked a great deal about you personally living out the change you want to see happen. The primary way Jesus created tension for change was how He lived. His very example of life demonstrated the heart of God.

4. Before beginning this journey of leading change in your church, how was your approach to church and ministry different?

_____

_____

_____

_____

_____

_____

_____

5. What changes are you already seeing on your leadership team and/or in the circles of people you influence?

_____

_____

_____

_____

_____

_____

Preaching to the Crowd

We know Jesus preached to the crowd. A key component to your leadership team bringing about change is to include them in the vision of where you are headed when that vision is woven into the sermons. Whether or not you personally preach on Sunday, this has to be part of leading change. For your church to become a healthy body that makes biblical disciples in relational environments, you have to preach about it.

6. Place a checkmark beside the way your leadership team could "preach to the crowds" in your church.

_____ Weekend services
_____ Weekday services
_____ Sunday school classes
_____ Volunteer leadership rallies
_____ Staff/elder/deacon meetings
_____ Ministry events/gatherings

7. Review the four ways to paint the tension in your church. It is vital that your leadership team has clarity and unity on this matter. Summarize what you've learned and what should be done as you move forward.

_____

_____

_____

_____

_____

_____

_____

RALLY AROUND THE TENSION

Day 4

In times of crisis people will often rally to help each other. Complete strangers will stand next to each other to fill sand bags when a flood threatens their town. When a home is destroyed by fire, donations of clothing, food, and money pour in. When your leadership team paints the tension, shows the gaps, invites people to take ownership, vision-casts the direction, and then challenges people to rally around the problem, the response can be incredible!

Seeing Solutions

To rally, people have to see solutions. Much like in a tragic crisis, when people can see why they're needed or what they can do, they will rally to help. By this time in the workbook you have solutions to help your church become a disciple-making church.

1. Which solutions could your team present to the church to help them rally?

_____

_____

_____

_____

_____

_____

_____

Maybe you listed some things like "encourage people to become involved in small groups or become more involved in the ministry of the church." You may also have listed ways people can help create a more relational environment within the church. Your list should reflect the values that will help create change in your church.

Laying out the Plan

At Real Life Ministries, we had to change how we did missions as we became more involved in our ministry in Ethiopia. To help create change, our volunteers—as well as the congregation—needed to see how we were going to reach our vision there. So a key step for us was to lay out our strategic plan. Not all at once, but in pieces so they could begin connecting the vision to how and what we were going to do. This led to increased commitment and buy-in.

2. Which of the specific strategic plans your team is discussing need to be revealed to the volunteers and church body?

_____

_____

_____

_____

_____

These strategic plans should be clear and intentional so people can understand quickly and easily. Also, we recommend that you present your plans in ways that allow people to discuss them and ask questions.

How they can play!

So often leadership teams leave out how to get the people involved. We have discussed in great detail to this point how to build teams and invite people to get involved. This must go beyond staff and volunteer teams. The entire church body—yes, even those who just take up seats—must be given opportunity to play a part in the overall change. Doing so will be key in helping you get those bench warmers into the game.

Below is a list of ways people can get involved. Use this list as a springboard to create your own.

- Join a small group.
- Begin giving financially.
- Start serving in a ministry.
- Attend membership and "what is discipleship" classes.

3. What ideas can you add to this list?

_____

_____

_____

_____

_____

By giving people some solutions to the problem, a clear strategic plan, as well as places to become a part, you will rally them around the tension. The buy-in to actually change grows within the church. Ownership for the change spreads.

REVIEW AND GROUP DISCUSSION

Day 5

Pray

Begin your time together in prayer.

Scripture

We established a foundation in week 1, identified the cultural shift and critical turning point in week 2, and looked forward to the desired "end" last week. Today, we will see how Nehemiah's God-given vision was put into action among the people.

Allow everyone a few minutes to read silently Nehemiah 3:1-32.

Key Points

♦ A clear and redundant pattern reveals a simple yet powerful truth. What phrase or ideas were repeated every few verses in chapter 3? ("Next to them" a person or people "made repairs" in a particular area.)

♦ Teams (small groups) were empowered to carry out specific work.

♦ The people knew their specific roles and took ownership of clear tasks.

Scripture here points to a job that is large and requires many people working together to finish. Successfully completing the task demands everyone on the team being equally committed and unified—not to mention an incredible amount of accurate communication. The communication must not only be clear to the people on the front lines but also be received by leadership when issues arise. Leadership also must be able to communicate through hurdles relationally and be able to ultimately encourage the entire team to move together.

The Week in Review

Discuss the major points and questions of each day, revisiting anything you may have marked throughout the week for group discussion. Share honestly about where God is challenging and encouraging you. Make sure your group environment is one of mutual respect, tempering observations and responses with grace. Time will not allow you to discuss all the questions, but visit the milestones and make sure each group member has an opportunity to offer input.

Day 1: Power of Invitation/You Can't Do It Alone
Day 2: Creating Chemistry
Day 3: Painting the Tension
Day 4: Rallying Around the Tension

Personal "Shifts" As a Disciple

What Is God teaching you about Himself? About yourself? About this church?

Week 4 Takeaways

What key truths, principles, and/or insights will you take away from this week's experience?

Action Steps

What action steps will you prayerfully consider based on this week's experience? Remember, be patient to let God fully develop your action plan. Resist the urge to jump into action immediately. You will revisit these in week 8 to formalize a clear plan of action for leading the *DiscipleShift* within your context.

Setup for Next Week

Building support is vital in leading our church in her God-given mission. Unity, by definition, will require wisdom in handling conflict. This next week, we delve into the principles and practices for proactively dealing with potential resistance to change. Anticipating areas and people requiring extra attention and tact will greatly quicken and strengthen the process of change. The result will be a healthier church.

overcoming obstacles

It has been said that church would be much easier if it weren't for the people in it. At times leaders in the church can feel this way, especially when it comes to dealing with change. Very few people like change, and nothing can discourage a leadership team faster than that one naysayer in the body. Oftentimes we see leadership teams really bog down due to people who have come against the change.

When leading change, you must acknowledge that there will be resistance. It's a fact! Not only are people sometimes just difficult, we mustn't forget that Satan hates what you do. Spiritual warfare is real, and leading your church to becoming healthier in making biblical disciples of Jesus Christ will stir up all kinds of problems. You must recognize it, believe it, and hit it head on. Any movement is going to have a squeaky wheel, so we have to know how to identify and fix the problem. We have seen many instances of the squeaky wheels becoming the most helpful cogs in the engine. When that happens, the unified direction is almost unstoppable.

Day 1

PREPARE THE WAY

Now that you have a good idea of who to approach to build your dream team, we need to look at a few cautions. First, the team needs to have power behind it. If others are constantly giving direction and micromanaging from the sidelines, the group will have a hard time forming as a true team. Church leadership built this team, so let the group go out there and perform as a team! At this point in the game you don't need anyone else saying, "Well, this is what I would have done." Second, this team needs to be supported from below too. Church leadership should be prepared to clear the path throughout of potential hurdles and roadblocks. Roadblocks can be people or a lack of resources and administrative support. Leadership needs to be ready to execute an action plan in place to make this happen even before this team meets for the first time.

Is church leadership committed to giving the team the authority it will need to lead this change? What conversations or actions need to take place to give them this credibility?

_____

_____

_____

_____

_____

What potential hurdles or roadblocks need to be addressed by leadership to help this team in the future?

_____

_____

_____

_____

_____

In those days when the number of disciples was increasing, the Hellenistic Jews among them complained against the Hebraic Jews because their widows were being overlooked in the daily distribution of food. So the Twelve gathered all the disciples together and said, "It would not be right for us to neglect the ministry of the word of God in order to wait on tables. Brothers and sisters, choose seven men from among you who are known to be full of the Spirit and wisdom. We will turn this responsibility over to them and will give our attention to prayer and the ministry of the word."

This proposal pleased the whole group. They chose Stephen, a man full of faith and of the Holy Spirit; also Philip, Procorus, Nicanor, Timon, Parmenas, and Nicolas from Antioch, a convert to Judaism. They presented these men to the apostles, who prayed and laid their hands on them.

So the word of God spread. The number of disciples in Jerusalem increased rapidly, and a large number of priests became obedient to the faith.

(Acts 6:1-7)

A biblical model of a good team launch is found in Acts 6. The church was growing rapidly, which is a good problem to have. However, the more people you have, the more rumblings you are going to have about various topics. This was the case for the apostles as a group of people began squawking about racial favoritism of benevolence to widows. This was a large task for the apostles to take on in addition to what they already had on their collective plates. Read Acts 6:1-7 and answer the questions below.

The apostles decided this was a problem that needed to be solved, but doing so would take their team from what they were called to do. How has your church leadership chased the "new thing" at times?

_____
_____
_____
_____
_____

This team was assembled and given authority by the apostles. Then their commission was communicated to the "group." What is your plan for communicating to the congregation the existence and mission of the dream team for change?

_____
_____
_____
_____
_____

Getting more people into leadership gives new people a place to play and mature in Christ. Reading farther in the chapter on your own, how do we know that Stephen was maturing?

_____
_____
_____
_____
_____

Getting Help from Outside

One of the most famous hotels in the west is the El Cortez in San Diego. The apartment hotel is famous for many reasons, but one in particular is the outside glass elevator. The "Starlight Express" was the first and only one of its kind in 1956. This elevator was not the creative brainchild of hotel executives or engineers. The idea came from a bellboy.

The legend is that all of the officials were outside the hotel trying to figure out a way to build an elevator to the restaurant dance club on the fourteenth floor called the Starlight Room. They wanted to give the club's patrons a convenient way to reach the club without bothering the guests of the hotel. Also, the hotel owner, Harry Handlery, didn't want to spend money on major structural changes or shut down the El Cortez during construction. The group was about ready to give up on the project when one of the hotel bellboys walked by and said, "Build the elevator on the outside of the hotel." The group was able to hear from an outside perspective and move to action.

Outside Perspective

Sometimes when we are working on a project for a period of time we get increasingly stuck. Ideas come less frequently and labor increases as productivity stalls. One solution many of us rely on is stepping away to clear our heads. We just have to set the project aside for a while—get a cup of coffee, mow the lawn, and so on. Most times when we get back to work we are far more productive. When stepping away doesn't work, we may ask others who aren't as close to the problem to help us solve it. Sometimes we need an expert or experienced perspective, so we attend a conference or go through a workbook like this one.

Where do you go for an outside perspective?

_____

_____

_____

_____

_____

_____

The outside perspective can be very helpful in keeping us productive. As in the case of the El Cortez and the Starlight Express, we have learned to get another perspective.

More People and More Energy

As we will discuss in detail in week 6, the more you communicate what the win is and show results of healthy change, the more likely three particular things are to happen: opposition, more people and more energy, and aligning existing ministries.

When new people come to you with new ideas and different perspectives, how do (or will) you and your team respond?

- Ignore the person and the idea.
- Argue with the person as you fight for your original idea.
- Listen, but don't do anything about the idea.
- Get frustrated that the Lord didn't already show you the right idea.
- Take the idea and get this person on the team to help you lead healthy change.

You could have actually checked all the responses, because we all react in less-than-ideal ways occasionally. But clearly the right answer is the last one. It sometimes can be difficult to adapt quickly and respond in a healthy manner to a new idea. We have most likely already invested a lot of time and energy into our current strategy for change. To possibly throw it out or start over because of a new idea seems wasteful.

We also have a hard time changing our plan for new ideas because we have attached the pathway to change to our own self-worth. Our pride gets in the way, and we don't want to have to give credit to the people around us—especially the new person with the new ideas. Another reason we don't want to ask a new person on the team is because we are worried about the feelings of the people who have been on the team from the beginning. We could also be worried about our own position, fearing that this new person may have more talent, intelligence, and experience.

Solution

All of these scenarios are real or could be real in your situation. The tension needs to be communicated and exposed through relationship. You and your team need to talk about these possible roadblocks as you continue to lead healthy change in your environment.

What are some hurdles your team may have with letting new ideas or new people join the team?

_____

_____

_____

_____

_____

_____

As you communicate fears you and others may have of letting others join the team, you and your team will experience more unity and alignment moving forward. If your team agrees to let new people and ideas in, it can be the difference between leading healthy change or a lot of your own time and energy wasted.

Day 2

REMOVE THE BARRIERS

So often when we work with churches we see their eyes light up with hope of accomplishing the vision of becoming a disciple-making church. Then that light quickly fades when the reality of overcoming barriers hits them. They often see no way around the problems. Often ministries, church organizational structures, or individuals within the church have become huge barriers to growth. This is when leadership teams must leverage tension most. The women's quilting ministry that has been in the church for 125 years may be a huge obstacle, but the tension that is created by not becoming a disciple-making church must help you press forward. So, the bottom line is how do we remove the ministry or structural issue that hangs around our necks like a biblical millstone that drags us to the bottom of the sea?

People

Let's deal with the toughest one first. Often our most difficult barrier is a person or group. That is why we're spending this entire week learning how to deal with people. Today we want to challenge you to begin thinking about how you will overcome people who are against change.

1. Rate this barrier in difficulty on a scale from 1 to 5 (1 being low and 5 being very high). Write two or three sentences describing how you came up with this rating. (Be prepared to share your answers with your group.)
Rating:_____

Why did you rate it that way?

_____

_____

_____

_____

_____

_____

Often churches build a culture around their difficult people. Sometimes, to keep a church from spontaneously combusting, the loudest, strongest personality gets what he or she wants. Sometimes difficult subjects are not discussed, so conflict is avoided altogether.

2. Place a checkmark next to the statement(s) that describes your environment when dealing with difficult people.

_____ a. Avoid conflict at all cost.
_____ b. Complain about it, but never really do anything.
_____ c. We have conflict, but never solutions.
_____ d. We ask difficult people to leave; dealing with them is just too hard.
_____ e. None of the above; we work very well with difficult people.

So which are you? From this exercise you can reflect on the kind of environment you have created. Write a brief summary of how your leadership team deals with difficult people. (Be prepared to discuss your answers in your group.)

_____
_____
_____
_____
_____
_____

Ministries

As a leader you have to take an honest look at which ministries you have that are not effective at making disciples. If you see that they are simply a barrier, then you must have the frank, honest, and loving conversations that remove these ministries. Each year at RLM we ask these questions about each ministry: "Is this ministry positively impacting our mission to make biblical disciples? If so, what fruit do we see?" Sometimes a ministry in our church just needs to be altered or refocused rather than totally removed. If that is the case, then again leadership must make the appropriate changes.

3. Use the chart below to evaluate some of your ministries. Write the name of the ministry in the first column. Then place an X in the column that best describes what you believe needs to happen with that ministry. Use the chart to help create a discussion within your leadership team on your perspective of current ministries.

Ministry	Keep it Currently doing a good job of impacting.	Change It It has a high value but needs some changes.	Cut It It has little to no value and only takes away from our effort.

4. Look at the "Change It" column. Hopefully several of your ministries fall into this category. Below we provided an opportunity to flesh some of this out. In as much detail as you can, write the changes you believe need to happen with these ministries.

Name of Ministry: _____

Changes to Make: _____
_____
_____
_____
_____
_____

Name of Ministry: _____
Changes to Make: _____

_____

_____

_____

_____

_____

_____

Name of Ministry: _____
Changes to Make: _____

_____

_____

_____

_____

_____

_____

Name of Ministry: _____
Changes to Make: _____

_____

_____

_____

_____

_____

_____

THE PROBLEM HAS A FIRST AND LAST NAME

Day 3

We were working with a long-established church, rooted in old programs and a strong resistance to change. God had sent a new young pastor (we will call him Dave) and some new families who were passionate about the church growing in relational discipleship. They wanted to start small groups. Several from our team traveled to meet with them and speak to the "leadership" about making the necessary changes to become a stronger disciple-making church. Before we arrived, we had a conference call with Dave. After several questions about the commitment level and buy-in from the key leadership team, he assured us that everyone was "bought in" and there would be no problems. He told us the whole team was "on fire"! Boy, was that more true than he knew.

For our meeting with the team, we sat around tables. Brandon was challenging the group to lead by example and get into small groups themselves, and the more he talked about this change in their environment the poorer the body language became with the chairman of the elders. Then suddenly the elder slammed his hand on the table and with a fiery red face said, "If you think I am going to get in a group and share my life with anyone, you're crazy and this isn't even godly! I study the Bible every day; I don't need anyone telling me how to walk with Jesus!" He then stood up and stormed out of the room, slamming the door behind him.

Everyone from our team, with startled looks on our faces, turned to Dave. Head down, he mumbled, "I was afraid Bill might react that way."

1. What were some obvious mistakes the senior pastor made that created the volatile situation?

_____

_____

_____

_____

_____

_____

One of Dave's classic mistakes was assuming everyone was in agreement. Clearly, he did not have heart-to-heart discussions with some of his key leaders. In fact, we learned later that Dave had avoided talking to Bill altogether out of fear of his reaction. He'd hoped that Bill's opposition would be resolved in our meeting. He knew about the problems and saw the potential for disunity. Churches rarely split from the bottom up. Typically they split from the top down. Disunity in leadership, as in Dave's church, is a classic scenario of what leads to an eventual church split. As a team leading change, you must recognize that creating this change is a spiritual, relational, and organizational battle. Refusing to confront these issues can lead to church division.

2. Fill in the blanks to the statement below:
"Churches rarely split from the _____.
Typically they split from the _____."

3. Read John 17:20-21. Summarize Jesus' prayer.

_____

_____

_____

_____

_____

_____

Jesus prayed for us in His church to live in unity. To maintain unity we must work through the relational issues that arise. As we have said and as you probably have experienced, organizational change usually strains relationships.

RLM has been in a state of constant change from day one. We have had to walk our leadership teams through change more times than we can remember. Sometimes we've been successful, and sometimes we've experienced significant bumps along the way. Every time we had issues, they were due to not identifying the people who were having problems with the change and evaluating their level of influence in the organization.

Take a moment to evaluate your environment. Think about the people who may be resistant to change. Starting at the top of the organization and working down, list their names and rate their level of influence from 1 to 5 (5 being a very high level of influence and 1 being very low). Also write the name of the person from your leadership team who has the best relationship to meet face-to-face with the individual who is resistant to change.

My prayer is not for them alone. I pray also for those who will believe in me through their message, that all of them may be one, Father, just as you are in me and I am in you. May they also be in us so that the world may believe that you have sent me.

(John 17:20-21)

Name	Level of influence	Person who should meet with them

4. Be prepared to share your answers to the following four questions within your group at the end of the week.

A. Who in your church do you think is the most resistant to change and why?

_____

_____

_____

_____

_____

_____

B. What cultural or environmental changes do you believe need to be made in your church to help those who most resist change?

_____

_____

_____

_____

_____

_____

C. When will you begin working with those who are resistant to the changes you are making?

_____

_____

_____

_____

_____

_____

D. How can you pray for them? Write out a specific prayer for those you listed in your chart. Pray for their hearts to be open to the changes God is leading your church in.

_____

_____

_____

_____

_____

_____

Day 4

DEAL WITH THE PROBLEM

Ignoring the problem will not make it go away. In fact, the problem will only get worse. As we demonstrated in the story yesterday, Dave did not deal with the problem in a face-to-face, relational way. To effectively lead change, the core leadership team must seek out and chase after those who do not agree with the change. This principle will accomplish two things for you if done properly. First, it will help you understand what the objections are to the change. Second, it will help you care for people who do not understand the change.

Often leadership in churches can take on the view that those opposed are the "bad" ones or the divisive people. Now, it is true that people who oppose moving forward can take on a divisive attitude, but in our experience this attitude often comes from how the leaders are communicating the change and relating to the body, not the other way around. There are two simple, but not always easy, things we challenge you to do: Seek them out and value their perspective.

Seek Them Out.

In yesterday's assignment you began to fill out the chart by adding the names of those in your church who may oppose the change you are moving toward. You also identified the influence they have in your church. How you go about communicating with each of these people is also vital to moving forward.

1. Below is a list of ways you could contact these people. Place an X by the method you think would be best.

_____ Type an email that communicates the change and the vision behind it. Then send it, telling those opposed how the church is moving forward.

_____ Type a letter that communicates the change and the vision behind the change. Then mail it to those opposed to the change.

_____ Address this group publically in a sermon, convincing them of the change and how great things will be because of the change.

_____ Set up face-to-face meetings in an informal setting to hear their concerns and allow them to ask questions.

Hopefully you placed an X by only the last option. Emails and letters can be helpful, supportive ways to communicate with people in the church, but they can at times cause more damage than help. Emails can feel nonrelational because the recipients cannot ask questions or voice their concerns. Certainly addressing the group publically will cause major division and could hurt people even more. To bring about change you have to handle each part in a relational way. Face-to-face is by far the best option. This allows you to hear the concerns, share your heart, and in a relational way talk through the direction God is leading your church.

Take time to reflect on your environment. In the first few weeks of this workbook you evaluated the environment that exists in your church. So take some time to answer the next few questions and bring forward what you have learned.

2. What has your team learned about your environment that will help you have a successful conversation with those you seek out?

_____
_____
_____
_____
_____
_____
_____

3. What has existed in your church environment in the past that would cause those opposed to the change to be hesitant to meet with you?

_____
_____
_____
_____
_____
_____
_____

Value Their Perspective.

Do you actually care what those who are struggling with the directional change are thinking? Are you approachable? Do you value the perspective that a naysayer might bring? As a leader in your church, how you answer those questions will impact how successfully your organization walks through change. Many leaders make the mistake of underestimating this process and devaluing the perspective of those against the change. Often leaders confuse valuing a perspective with agreeing with the perspective. Just because you value their input does not mean you will agree with it and implement it.

4. Fill in the blanks

"Often, leaders confuse _____ a perspective
with _____ with the perspective."

You should have used the terms valuing and agreeing. Again valuing a person's perspective does not mean that you agree. Below are specific points that you can implement in your face-to-face meetings that can help you value someone's perspective.

5. Place a C next to the ways of valuing others' perspectives you consistently implement, place an S next to the ones you somewhat use, and place an R next to the ones you rarely use.

_____ **Ask open-ended questions.** Start your conversations with "what" and "how" questions: How long have you felt that way? What happened that caused you to believe that? What did you hear when we announced that? These kinds of questions cause you, the listener, to be curious about them and try to understand.

_____ **Repeat back what you heard.** Vital to valuing what someone says is repeating what you heard them say to validate their words. Do not fill in the blanks for them. So, what I hear you saying is . . . (repeat their actual words). This communicates to the person that you care and are hearing them.

_____ **Take notes.** To show that you value their perspective, write it down. Then repeat back to them what you wrote to both make sure you heard correctly and also to demonstrate that you value what they are saying. It is also helpful to take this information to the team to share any ideas that are pertinent to help you lead.

_____ **Share what God is doing with you.** Leaders often underestimate the power of their personal testimony of what God is doing with them. Share with the person what God is teaching you and connect it to the vision of what God is doing corporately. Be willing to be transparent with your own failures.

_____ **Identify specific objectives.** Make sure to identify specific objectives from the conversation that you both agree on. You want to hear them and ask them for what they want as a goal from the meeting. Share with them what you hope to gain from your time together.

_____ **Ask for permission.** Leaders often want to skip right to their part and just convince the person they are meeting with that the leader is right and the individual is wrong. Before sharing anything—vision, testimony, or even correcting a specific point they may have incorrect information about—ask for permission to share your thoughts. Again, this values the person you are meeting with.

_____ **Prayer.** This may seem obvious, but prayer must be present. At both the beginning and the end of your meeting spend time in prayer together. Ask for specific requests from the person and give this time to the Lord.

6. List the items that you marked with an R. How will you change those to Cs or Rs in your upcoming meetings? (Be prepared to share your answers with your group.)

_____

_____

_____

_____

_____

_____

Finally, we are going to practice the two skills above that we can replicate in a workbook. Below is a scenario of a person you might meet with. After you read the scenario, read the list of possible questions you could ask in the meeting. Place an X next to the question that would help you best understand the person you are meeting with.

A senior pastor hears from a staff person that a key volunteer (John) in the church is opposed to any changes with the church philosophy. John has served at the church and in the business world. He has typically been very supportive in the past, but the changes that are being presented are just "rubbing him the wrong way." The staff person tells the senior pastor that John just seems upset and he thinks John wants to just leave the church without "causing a problem." So the pastor pursues John by setting up a meeting over coffee.

Which questions would you choose to ask in the above scenario?

A. _____ John, I know you are upset, but are you going to buy in to the vision of our church?
B. _____ What has happened or been said that has caused you concern?
C. _____What frustrations do you have that are not being addressed?
D._____ Are you going to get onboard with the changes?
E. _____ Where did we as a church miscommunicate or do something that left you feeling this way?
F. _____ Do you think you are just being unreasonable?

In the questions above you should have placed an X next to B, C, and E. The other three options are closed questions that do not show any concern for John's input. Asking closed questions may cause a person to feel shut out or that an ultimatum is being given. Good, open-ended questions encourage John to give his input and to be involved in the process. The next step, though, is to actually listen to the response the person gives.

Repeat back what you heard.

When we ask good questions, we want to capture what is said back to us. We want the person we are talking with to feel heard. (This can also help us remember what they've said and stay focused in the moment instead of rushing to our next point.) Often when churches lead change, the people who are against the change or have questions just want to know that the leadership is hearing them. The skill of listening in our culture is a lost art. People need to be heard! Hearing is often equated with valuing. When you meet with someone you must value the person and listen to what he or she has to say.

7. People need to be_____!

To best help people feel heard, you'll want to repeat back to them what they've said. Look them in the eyes and validate that you have heard them. Using the scenario of the pastor meeting with John, we have given some examples of how a good listener would respond to a statement.

John: I just think all of this change is happening too fast, and I don't understand how we are going to actually implement these ideas in the ministry of our church.
Senior Pastor: Okay, John, so what I'm hearing you say is that you feel we are moving too fast and you're not sure how we will implement these ideas. Is that accurate?
John: Yes, that is what I am saying.
Senior Pastor: Wow, John, thanks for telling me how you feel. It's important to me to hear you.

Notice John's statement was not changed, nor did the senior pastor try to sway him in any direction. He just repeated John's concern. Now, John's perspective may or may not be completely accurate. The pastor may need to fill in some blanks for John. The two will continue to dialogue, but before they could move forward the pastor had to value and hear what John was saying.

8. Think of someone you know who is a great listener. When you talk to this person, you really feel like he or she "hears you." In your opinion, what does this individual do that makes him or her a good listener in a face-to-face conversation?

_____

_____

_____

_____

_____

_____

_____

REVIEW AND GROUP DISCUSSION

Day 5

Pray

Begin your time together in prayer.

Scripture

Enlist three volunteers to read Nehemiah 4:1-8, 9-15, and 16-23.

Key Points

- Not only was everyone in the community not supportive of the positive changes, some were outright opposed.
- (4:1-8) Sanballat furiously tried to influence public opinion and discourage the people through mockery, conspiracy, and disturbances. (Lies and false rumors were also created to threaten Nehemiah later in 6:1-14.)
- (4:9-23) The threefold strategy for overcoming obstacles was prayer, perseverance, and proactivity.
- Nehemiah's plan ensured that progress continued while they dealt with opposition. Even prevention of serious threats or likely disturbances was not allowed to distract the people's attention from the primary goal.

Nehemiah had built support from leaders and people in the community. But just because God is at work and a leader is acting wisely does not mean resistance and opposition will not be faced. In fact, more intense opposition may be experienced, but by the grace of God, the obstacles will be overcome.

The hardest part of transitioning is not a matter of program but people. Relationships are what ministry is all about, but they can get messy. Are we willing to dig in deep personally in order to see meaningful ministry rather than just religious activities?

The Week In Review

Discuss the major points and questions of each day, revisiting anything you may have marked throughout the week for group discussion. Share honestly about where God is challenging and encouraging you. Make sure your group environment is one of mutual respect, tempering observations and responses with grace. Time will not allow you to discuss all the questions, but visit the milestones and make sure each group member has an opportunity to offer input.

Day 1: Prepare the Way
Day 2: Remove the Barriers
Day 3: The Problem Has a First and Last Name
Day 4: Dealing with the Problem

Personal "Shifts" As a Disciple

What is God teaching you about Himself? About yourself? About this church?

_____

_____

_____

_____

_____

Week 5 Takeaways

What key truths, principles, and/or insights will you take away from this week's experience?

_____

_____

_____

_____

_____

Action Steps

What action steps will you prayerfully consider based on this week's experience? Remember, be patient to let God fully develop your action plan. Resist the urge to jump into action immediately. You will revisit these in week 8 to formalize a clear plan of action for leading the *DiscipleShift* within your context.

_____

_____

_____

_____

_____

Setup for Next Week

Any shift requires extra effort up front. Once something is in motion, it is easier to keep moving. But it is still important to direct the right energy toward its progress. These laws apply not only in the physical world but also in the social realm. Now that we have specifically targeted steps in building unity and overcoming resistance, how will we harness the power of momentum? The days leading to our next discussion will identify key principles in the secret to momentum: creating and communicating goals.

SMART goals and momentum

Any shift requires extra effort up front. Once something is in motion, it is easier to keep moving. But it is still important to direct the right energy toward its progress. These laws apply not only in the physical world but also in the social realm. Now that you have specifically targeted steps in building unity and overcoming resistance, how will you harness the power of momentum? This week we will identify key principles in the secret to momentum: creating and communicating goals.

The habit of success will build momentum, carrying your church forward through each new challenge towards a culture that is forever focused on making disciples of Jesus.

Day 1

EATING THE ELEPHANT

We have all heard the riddle, "How do you eat an elephant?" There is real wisdom in the answer, which of course is "one bite at a time." We tend to forget this when we are leading people toward a goal that will change future impact in ministry. Often we wrongly focus on describing the elephant's massive size or origin instead of the benefit of a full stomach. Your clarity of vision is what keeps you motivated. A vision of completion keeps people from becoming intimidated or overwhelmed. Most people in any community or organization, including the church, need smaller goals to keep them running the race that will eventually lead to the big goal.

Imagine how it felt to be one of Noah's sons, building the ark. Noah, as your leader, has continually cast vision about a flood caused by rain that you have never seen before. It would have been very difficult to "keep your eyes on the prize" as you sweat over your Cyprus wood. This is the position we put our people in when we expect them to be diligent without seeing small changes being made. Instead, we want them to recognize the progress of "small victories" after every section constructed and every new species gathered, so to speak.

While trying to achieve a goal, have you ever used one of these smaller goals?

- ☐ Weigh regularly when you're on a diet.
- ☐ Make a daily reading plan when you want to read through the Bible.
- ☐ Break a home repair project into smaller tasks.
- ☐ Save small amounts from every paycheck to accumulate enough money for a large purchase.

After some thought, you would agree that large goals and projects are all just a compilation of smaller tasks built upon each other. In fact, smaller goals are essential to success. One benefit of smaller wins is that they help to motivate. Seeing progress is a great way to encourage the people doing the heavy lifting on a project, especially when the progress is celebrating the completion of a short-term win. The completion of short-term wins also gives momentum, which motivates more people to join the excitement. Some of the people you considered your biggest obstacles will change their view in order to be a part.

Another benefit to short-term wins is that they give you a chance to make small corrections to the overall strategy. We don't know what we don't know when we're first developing a strategy. Through real-time evaluation of short-term wins we can gather valuable information.

Ultimately, we'll see next week that shifting the direction of your church (or any organization) is about changing its culture. So when you think about all that goes into a culture—tradition, stories of events, and moments shared through relationships—generating smaller wins becomes essential to leading a change in culture because you are creating new memories and new shared experiences. These memories are the glue that holds relationships together and the essential building blocks to culture.

Now, in order to generate smaller wins we first have to break down the overall change into important, unique steps. Fill in the blanks with your best guess and be prepared to share your answers with your group.

What is the overall change that you would like to see accomplished in your ministry or area of leadership (the elephant)?

_____

_____

_____

_____

_____

_____

Break down your goal into ten steps that have to happen before you can reach that goal. (This may sound easy, but after you go over this part with your group you will probably all have different steps.)

Step 1. _____

Step 2. _____

Step 3. _____

Step 4. _____

Step 5. _____

Step 6. _____

Step 7. _____

Step 8. _____

Step 9. _____

Step 10. _____

In the coming days we will go over this list, and you can start to shape these steps into your smaller wins to lead your church or organization through change. This amount of preparation may seem tedious, but in the long run this preparation can be the difference between creating healthy change and hamstringing the entire body. It is vital that you don't skip this step.

We'll offer one last thought about mapping out your plan. When I (Lance) was in college I took a class on how to start a small business; the final exam was a business plan. Most of the students chose businesses they made up to research for their business plans. I was just young and dumb enough to start my own business, so this business plan was going to be what I took to the bank to get a loan. I worked and worked on this business plan, and I thought I had everything covered to be a success right out of college. My professor told me that every business takes twice as long and twice the money as the business plan estimates for it to be profitable. I was sure that wouldn't be the case with my plan. Five months later I was headed back home with my tail between my legs. My professor was absolutely right, and if I had gone back and reworked the numbers on my business plan I would have made a go of it. The point of that story is that when you are ready to make your move, it's always better to take another closer look at your conclusions—especially when it comes to leading change. You don't know how many opportunities you will have to make this *DiscipleShift* at your church. If you do it wrong the first time, you may actually make it harder to get the church to move in the future.

BODIES IN MOTION

Day 2

Before we start creating short-term wins, you'll want to fully understand the benefits for your church to create and communicate short-term wins. There are four: momentum, risk management, healthy alignment, and proof for detractors.

Momentum

Newton's law of motion states that bodies in motion will stay in motion. Newton also proved that an object at rest will stay at rest unless an unbalanced force acts upon it. Unfortunately, this is also true of churches at rest, particularly if a congregation hasn't had to deal with any significant change for a period of time.

Recently I heard a pastor refer to his congregation as the "Frozen Chosen," which is funny and yet sad because of its truth. But before we start to point fingers at the congregation about their lack of motivation, we need to understand our role as leaders. Have we as leaders allowed our churches at rest to stay that way because we have not led to the point of creating a tension, or "unbalanced force"?

As we continue to look at adding short-term wins to your overall change plan, we must consider the first benefit—momentum. Creating and communicating short-term wins provides the unbalanced force necessary to slowly thaw the frozen chosen. The more motion goes into the church, the easier time it has moving in the direction of change. The more momentum the church has, the more you can become part of the change and the less leadership has to push. Wouldn't it be great if you could be a part of a culture that changes the church into what it was designed to be? It would be a church that not only thaws but starts to really heat up, a church that is making disciples through relationship, and a church that grows more and more to be the bride of Christ.

Creating and communicating short-term wins is essential for success in creating healthy change in your church. The first benefit of short-term wins is _____.

Risk Management

Another benefit to short-term wins is risk management for your church. If you didn't do short-term wins and tried to change the church, you would struggle to succeed. The entire church would be in shock, and the people would feel confused and distrustful of leadership. Think about Newton's law again. Here is a body (your church) that has been at rest for a period of time. Now, without a warning, it gets thrust forward! It would feel like the church had been hit by a tornado!

Everyone, even the most progressive person, struggles with change to a certain degree. We as shepherds should always be cognizant of the needs, desires, and fears of the sheep. With that in mind, a good shepherd wouldn't force the church to automatically accept the change without any warning. Creating and clearly communicating short-term wins gives people a gentle way to not only get used to change but also an opportunity to contribute.

The second benefit to creating short-term wins is _____ for your church.

And they devoted themselves to the apostles' teaching and the fellowship, to the breaking of bread and the prayers. And awe came upon every soul, and many wonders and signs were being done through the apostles. And all who believed were together and had all things in common. And they were selling their possessions and belongings and distributing the proceeds to all, as any had need. And day by day, attending the temple together and breaking bread in their homes, they received their food with glad and generous hearts, praising God and having favor with all the people. And the Lord added to their number day by day those who were being saved.

(Acts 2:42-47, ESV)

125

Alignment

Creating short-term wins also gives your church body a chance to start to align with the upcoming change. The third benefit to short-term wins is alignment. The more short-term wins get accomplished and the more momentum starts to build, the more the church starts to align people, resources, and ministry.

Your behavior never lies about what your priorities are as a person. What you spend your time and resources on is truly where your heart is. "For where your treasure is, there your heart will be also" (Matthew 6:21, esv).

The same goes for an entire church body and how decisions are made within that body. Without alignment on priorities, the church spreads its resources too thin and the impact is minimized. Short-term wins give decision-makers from all over the church a chance to slowly align together toward healthy change.

The third benefit to short-term wins is _____ of church resources, people, and ministry.

Proof for Detractors

Last week we learned about addressing people at the church who oppose change. As the success starts to build from accomplishing one short-term win after another, the opposition is provided with proof. Hard, cold facts are the best way to change people's opinions, which is why the fourth benefit of creating short-term wins is proof for the detractors. Regardless of how entrenched people are about their particular position, they are going to soften when the number of wins starts to pile up.

The fourth benefit of creating short-term wins is_____.

Clearly creating and communicating short-term wins is an important and necessary part of creating healthy change at your church. Tomorrow we will begin to focus on how to shape your steps into short-term wins.

Running Downhill

Most kids who play outside have the opportunity to play on a hill. No matter the season, children will make very good use of the incline and decline. If you watch long enough, you'll see the children climb and then roll, run, and slide down, using the momentum of the decline to speed up their movements. Children love to run as fast as they can, and they laugh even though they might be a little out of control.

How do you describe momentum? Give an example of the power of momentum.

_____
_____
_____
_____
_____
_____
_____

As we lead healthy change in our environment, we can start to feel the same momentum we felt as children when we ran downhill. We start to compound the momentum of short-term wins, and it builds momentum through the entire organization. This energy, if it is harnessed, can make your challenge of leading change much easier. This week we are going to discover ways to multiply the momentum that is already building.

First of all, organization momentum is that "buzz" that seems to be what everybody is talking about. You need to make sure you are talking about the short-term wins you are witnessing. Create your own buzz. Talk about it everywhere. Talk about it to anyone who is part of your culture.

For a perspective on how much you're going to have to communicate, think about your favorite song from your favorite band. By the time you first heard the song on the radio, the band had already played it hundreds, if not thousands of times. The band is already sick of the song and can play the entire song with nothing more than muscle memory when you begin to hum along in your car.

You need to talk about your short-term wins _____
and to _____.

You should have written everywhere and to everyone. Determine to continue talking about the wins generated long enough for people within your circle of influence to get clarity on the coming change. Here's how you'll know if you and your team are communicating the wins enough. If people start to get clarity on the issue, then they will automatically respond. They may respond in a variety of ways, but they will respond. For example, one weekend Jim, our senior pastor, made a plea to our congregation for $6,000 for one of our missions after the offering plates had already been passed. The goal was to conduct a training event for pastors in Ethiopia, but many of the indigenous church leaders didn't have money to cover their travel. The vision was very specific and clear for our congregation. They responded by giving more than $50,000, and we have used that money to do many more things in Ethiopia.

This clarity that develops from succeeding at and communicating your short-term goals will lead to a response in three ways.

Response #1: Opposition

Even though conflict can be very difficult, it is a natural response to increasing clarity of a vision. The more people understand the direction of where they are being led, the more some will tend to fight. Many of these people might be in leadership of some kind. They might be long-time members and friends or supporters. This opposition to change should not come as a surprise; it is a part of leading. There is a strong chance that some of the people might choose their own comfort or preference over unity as a church.

Jesus had to deal with opposition from His own disciples too. Just when He was revealing to His disciples His plan, they left Him.

Aware that his disciples were grumbling about this, Jesus said to them, "Does this offend you? Then what if you see the Son of Man ascend to where he was before! The Spirit gives life; the flesh counts for nothing. The words I have spoken to you—they are full of the Spirit and life. Yet there are some of you who do not believe." For Jesus had known from the beginning which of them did not believe and who would betray him. He went on to say, "This is why I told you that no one can come to me unless the Father has enabled them." From this time many of his disciples turned back and no longer followed him.

(John 6:61-66)

Response #2: More People and More Energy

With clarity, momentum can easily be built and change made exponentially as people start to contribute. When people understand and hear a clear message, they will respond with their ideas, energy, and willingness to contribute. This week we will talk more about aligning and changing your timeline and strategy as new people and ideas come forward.

Response #3: Aligning Existing Ministries

With clarity, you also gain momentum as existing ministries join with the change initiative. Alignment of ministries can be a powerful catalyst to future change. Aligning ministries carefully and intentionally, which we will go over later this week, can result in a bigger and bigger positive energy storm that can make change happen quickly.

BE SMART

Day 3

Now that we have your elephant reduced to bite-sized steps, we need to refine the steps further by adding another filter to ensure good candidates for short-term wins.

SMART is an acronym that has been used in leadership for more than thirty years as a filter for creating short-term wins and goals. A good goal is:

S - Specific
M - Measurable
A - Attainable
R - Relevant
T - Timely

Specific

Being specific is vital in communication. No matter how passionate, unified, and focused the leadership, creating change can be a struggle if the win is not specific. Leadership must be able to communicate the short-term win in one phrase or sentence. For instance, a goal of "five new small groups by July" works. When the entire church hears that, they will know what the win is because it is specific. Churches are notorious for being vague with their vision, mission, and process. They seem to opt for more politically correct statements that don't offend anyone or risk anything. When a statement isn't offensive, however, often no one understands what it means and it doesn't challenge anyone to step up. Draw a line in the sand and go with the people who have the courage to step out.

Day 1 of this week you were asked to break your overall change into ten steps. Write any one of those steps you would like to eventually become a short-term win on the line below.

_____

_____

_____

_____

_____

_____

_____

Now ask yourself these questions to see if the step is indeed specific.

☐ Would someone be able to clearly communicate the win of this step?
☐ Is the step likely to generate a discussion about how to accomplish it?
☐ Would a team member have an easy time remaining apathetic after hearing the step?

Measurable

Your specific short-term win must also be measurable. Imagine a sporting event without a measurement for success. It would cease to be a sport at all; it would simply be activity. Consider a school, restaurant, business, or industry without measurable standards. Without measurements we wouldn't know if anyone or anything was succeeding or failing or how to make future adjustments.

If your short-term win is specific but the unit by which you measure success is vague, then there still will be confusion. The example "Five new small groups by July" is measurable. Everyone understands how many new small groups makes five. More importantly there is a time limit to establish the five new home groups. Take away either specific measure in that goal and it loses power. A deadline is key for clarity and for motivation.

Procrastination seems to be more prevalent than ever. You would think with all of the electronic devices we have at our disposal now that we would be more productive. There is no question that the Internet has made our world more productive, but it has also made it far easier to waste time . . . faster.

Think how many projects you have on your list to do at work, home, and in ministry. We constantly have to reshuffle our priorities to maintain effectiveness. One way we reprioritize our task list is based on urgency. What task needs to be done the soonest? If your short-term win does not have a deadline, the work that will make it happen will continually get pushed toward the bottom of the list. The short-term win has to have two units of measurement embedded in the statement. Usually an amount desired and an amount of time (a deadline) for the amount to be achieved.

Take the statement you've been refining and add the two units of measurement to it now.

_____

_____

_____

_____

_____

_____

It's scary to draw a line in the sand and tell people specifically what you would like to see accomplished. The fear of failure is so prevalent in our culture. What if it doesn't happen? What if you were too optimistic? What if . . . ? When you make the short-term win specific and measurable, you suddenly feel the pressure. You can already hear the familiar rumble of the Monday-morning quarterbacks. The sound of people giving their opinions after the dust settles about what they would have done differently and what you should have done.

This is why so many teams, churches, and organizations fail to make short-term wins and specific and measurable goals. The fear of failure and the resulting "I told you so" paralyzes the church, keeping it from making specific and measurable short-term wins.

Push through this tension. Setting a specific, measurable short-term win and goals actually serves to unify those who hear it. Because they easily understand what the win is, everyone starts to want to contribute. The church begins to align behind not your vision or the team's vision, but the entire church's collective vision that you have been able to communicate. Energy is renewed in the entire church. When everyone is on the same team striving and working to achieve short-term wins, there's no one left to be a Monday-morning quarterback.

Attainable

I (Lance) worked for a larger company that sold computer networking hardware to Fortune 500 companies. Every quarter, the quota for our bonuses would be set by the corporate office—and without consulting the sales team responsible for achieving the goal. Naturally, the number was high, because the people in charge wanted to see higher profits. Quarter after quarter the team grew less and less motivated as the goal got further out of reach. The carrot was too far in front of the donkey. The goal was not attainable.

As you look at your steps to get to your overall goal, ask yourself, "Is this specific, measurable short-term win attainable?" One very good way to find out if the short-term win is considered attainable by the people responsible to make it happen is to ask them. Remember, this is not a good time to use your skills to persuade! Listen to their feedback and make adjustments to increase or decrease the parameters of the short-term win in order to ensure it is attainable.

Below are some approaches you may want to use when presenting your short-term win to the people who will make it happen:

I was thinking that a first good milestone for us would be _____.
What do you think about that?
I would like to see us really stretch ourselves, but I want to make sure that it's a win for everyone. Do you think _____ would be out of the question?
I was thinking about communicating _____ as a short-term win to give us some momentum. Do you think that is too challenging or too "business as usual"?

One last reminder about making attainable short-term wins: the win still has to be a stretch for your team to accomplish. If is perceived as too easy, then even when you achieve the win you may still be the brunt of skepticism from people who are against the change.

Relevant

The word relevant has some baggage attached to it in church circles, so let's look at the term as it relates to how your short-term win aligns with your people, process, and plan. A short-term win must align with (be relevant to) your people. First, by "people" I mean the individuals who are working to make this change happen at your church; this is your change culture. Also, the short-term win should align with people outside the change culture who are still stakeholders at your church. If the win doesn't align with your people who are excited for the overall change, you will lose momentum. If the short-term win is not relevant to people on the outside of the change, their future buy-in with the change is at risk. In other words, it is hard for someone to want to "jump on the bandwagon" when they don't know if it is winning.

Is the short-term win relevant to your people both outside and inside the change-culture? If yes, then keep reading. If your answer is no, then look at your win statement and ask people some questions to further refine the statement. If their responses to the following questions don't align with the overall change, tweak your short-term win until it does.

> What would be some of the benefits to our church in accomplishing this win?
> When you hear _____, why do you think we would want to do that?
> Do you see how this step aligns with the overall change we're trying to accomplish?

The short-term win has to be relevant to the process. In day 1 of this week we broke down the overall change into smaller steps. Those smaller steps help to ensure that your short-term win is relevant to the process of creating the overall change. Your short-term win needs to be easily understood by all as a clear next step toward the overall goal.

Timely

We already went over how time is a key ingredient in making a short-term goal measurable. That is not what we mean by "timely," however. In this case timely means building a natural rhythm with the church toward change. You can build a rhythm in two crucial ways: macro and micro. Being timely at a macro level means your short-term wins don't all happen this month and then a year later you have another one. You need to space the short-term wins so there is a rhythm. People will start following then, because they are expecting it. So every month or quarter you're ready with another step, another short-term win, to communicate and celebrate.

Making short-term wins timely at a micro level is to build a rhythm of success for future change by meeting regularly with the people responsible for the change. Every week or two, you need to meet with the team to see how they are progressing on their personal tasks toward the short-term win and to encourage them. Also, during the meeting the team can be encouraged by each other as they hear progress happening toward accomplishing a short-term win.

TURNING A LOSS INTO A WIN

Day 4

With clarity on the win and proof starting to grow overwhelming with short-term successes the church is experiencing, the people who were either against change or not committed to change start to respond. Neutral and negative positions begin shifting toward positive. People start to respond typically in three ways. Put an R next to the responses we have gone over this week.

_____ Talking behind your back   _____ More people and more energy
_____ Starting their own team   _____ Aligning existing ministries
_____ Opposition   _____ Stonewalling
_____ Lobby leaders on the fence   _____ Leaving the church in anger

You should have put an R next to opposition, more people and more energy, and aligning existing ministries.

Opposition

As we discussed, even Jesus experienced people who opposed Him and His ministry. Sometimes we can't stay unified with those who oppose change. We discovered that people might easily have different passions than the rest of the church, and these feeling don't get exposed until you start to communicate what the "win" is for the church. When people realize that their unity with the church was based only on a lack of clarity in the vision of the church, they tend to leave. This is very difficult to experience. These are good people, friends, co-laborers, and you can remain in relationship with them. They just need to find another church body that has the same passion for their same mission.

Opposition is a necessary and healthy part of the change process.
This statement is (true or false) _____. Why?

_____

_____

_____

_____

_____

One of the many benefits to clarity in what is winning is that people who are not part of the healthy change will leave. This statement is true. If their passion for their ministry or event is greater than their willingness to be unified, you want to know immediately. Let them go in love, make it easy for them to return if they choose to, but let them go. This may end up being "winning by losing," or "addition by subtraction."

More People and More Energy

Another response to clarity of change happening in your church is new people wanting to join the shift and help.

Your willingness to add new people on the team and possibly adapting some of their new ideas will help/hurt you? (Circle one.)

The natural momentum of adding new people to your existing team only helps your chances of creating healthy change in your church. You can't lead healthy change using only your strategy and your team. You and your team are already onboard with the change, but you won't complete the change unless the entire organization is a part of it. If the team becomes exclusive and closed to others now, change will never happen.

Aligning Existing Ministries

We talked previously about how to use the 2x2 ministry matrix to align existing ministries. (See page 75 for a refresher, if needed.) In reference to that chart, we're going to look at how to change a "hobby" ministry into a "life's mission." The reason you would even try to salvage a hobby is because the passion for the ministry or event already exists. Simply, the ministry already has momentum, so why wouldn't you try to make some simple tweaks to align it and make it a life's mission?

The key to moving a current ministry or event from a hobby to a life's mission is to make changes that add profit. In our example, people are already very passionate about men's basketball, so how would we increase the profit (discipleship) to men's basketball?

Making small changes that over time will make a huge difference is key. For instance, we could have the team pray together before warm-ups and assign someone to bring a devotion. Maybe the guys will start to bring up issues for prayer that could carry relationship off the basketball court. Another thing that could make a big difference is encouraging the team to meet as a men's accountability group at a separate time and place. In that setting they would focus on challenging each other to grow spiritually in their relationship with the Lord and at home.

Men's basketball could turn into a huge kingdom win with some real impact in the lives and families of the men who participate. Some men would never feel comfortable joining a group if they didn't know someone there. As they build relationship on the basketball court, they can also build relationship with the men in their accountability group. In this way men's basketball with a few intentional changes has become uniquely profitable, far surpassing the original classification of hobby.

What If You Don't Win?

For most of this week we have been discussing the advantages to creating short-term wins, the advantages of momentum and alignment you gain when your church keeps achieving. What if you don't win?

No one should plan to lose. However, all is not lost if the team reached for a short-term win and didn't achieve it. There are some steps you can take that will help you win in the long run. In fact, you might look at a loss as a turning point to the team succeeding on its overall change goal. Some of our greatest losses and frustrations in ministry can be the times the Lord teaches us the most. What we consider a negative, in hindsight can be the most significant time for the Lord leading His church.

Step #1: Remember that God can turn our losses into wins for Him.

The apostle Paul spent well over 20 percent of his thirty-plus-year ministry in jail. He was unable to plant churches and travel to encourage, evangelize, and empower new leaders. Without a doubt this time of incarceration for advancing the kingdom was a huge frustration to him in many ways. However, without Paul's time in jail, we wouldn't have his letters to the Ephesians, Philippians, Colossians, and to Philemon. Paul was forced to write and give the churches that were sprouting up information that is true for all churches everywhere. These letters from his first imprisonment are Scriptures the church has now benefited from for almost two thousand years!

Step #2: Make adjustments to your original plan.

Imagine you are going to travel four hundred miles down a perfectly straight highway. You could put the car on cruise control and relax. But let's add one other factor to this scenario: your wheels are 2 percent out of alignment, and you refuse to move your steering wheel in order to compensate. That 2 percent discrepancy is not going to matter for the first twenty miles. However, if you don't start to make a correction with your steering, you are eventually going to be completely off the road and heading in the wrong direction! We don't live in a vacuum. There is zero chance that your team that is going to see this *DiscipleShift* happen at your church thought of 100 percent of the environmental variables and hurdles. We simply don't know what we don't know.

And we know that in all things God works for the good of those who love him, who have been called according to his purpose.

(Romans 8:28)

As information becomes apparent to the team, you are able to make corrections and calculate changes that will greatly increase the likelihood of you future success. You'll need to build into your schedule meetings that force the team to look objectively at the results from short-term wins regardless of the outcome.

Possible questions to talk over with the team:
   What did we learn while we were striving for this short-term win?
   Is the bar too high? Too low? Should we revise our overall goal for change to be more realistic?
   Should we revise how we are communicating the vision for change?
   Who should we add to the team? Do we have the right people in the right places?

Step #3: Communicate to turn that frown upside down.

Communication is essential to building momentum when the team starts to meet or exceed short-term goals. Communication is even more important, however, in the event that the team was too optimistic about their outcomes.

Every dark cloud has a silver lining. Look for it! Go and find the win story that happened as a direct result of the church striving toward the short-term win. Look for the win stories you can communicate with the entire church. Even the church's strongest opponent to change can be positively moved through a win story of personal impact.

When we were just getting home groups started at Real Life Ministries, we had a win story that rocked the church. One of the men from a home group came onstage and told how the group had reached out and helped his family in a unique way. His first child decided to come early, and he hadn't finished the basement or the nursery. So his home group, which included several men who were in construction, went to his house while the man and his wife were at the hospital and did the work for him. While he was onstage he started to cry about how humbling it was to have received this gift of service for his family. The few people there who weren't in home groups at that point wanted to sign up for one after that service! And that is just one of many stories.

Look for the story of personal impact and tell that story. Personal impact will motivate people, and it also greatly minimizes the fact that maybe the church didn't achieve the short-term win.

Here are places to look for win stories that make the most impact on leading healthy change in the future at your church:

- Someone who was impacted positively by the short-term win.
- A person who was against the change but recently converted.
- A member of your team who made a personal growth step.
- Anyone who witnessed growth because of the short-term goal.

REVIEW AND GROUP DISCUSSION

Day 5

Pray
Begin your time together in prayer.

Scripture
Choose three people to read Nehemiah 6:15-19, 7:1–7 and 7:66-73.

Key Points
- (6:16) Everyone, even critics, could see this work was done with God's help.
- (7:2-3) Nehemiah again demonstrated wisdom in leadership by delegating responsibility and empowering people.
- (7:2-3,5)Clearly defined tasks resulted in successful group ownership. In other words, a clear goal made an easier win.
- Nehemiah shifted the focus from the negative to the positive, from opposition to allies.
- (7:5-66) Genealogies may seem to be dry reading and typically easy to skip over in Scripture, but they are evidence that people matter to God. Numbering the people not only ascribed value to individuals but it also rallied and encouraged the collective community, making it easier to see where they had come from and focus on where they were headed.

We can never forget that change is not a one-time decision—change is a journey requiring everyone to take steps and leaps of faith along the way. It is essential to keep people motivated and encouraged with clear markers of progress and recognition of the lives being impacted and joining the movement. What greater thing could be said inside and outside of our church than that God is obviously at work and moving among us?

The Week In Review
Discuss the major points and questions of each day, revisiting anything you may have marked throughout the week for group discussion. Share honestly about where God is challenging and encouraging you. Make sure your group environment is one of mutual respect, tempering observations and responses with grace. Time will not allow you to discuss all the questions, but visit the milestones and make sure each group member has an opportunity to offer input.

Day 1: Eating the Elephant
Day 2: Bodies in Motion
Day 3: Working SMART
Day 4: Turning a Loss into a Win

Personal "Shifts" As a Disciple

What is God teaching you about Himself? About yourself? About this church?

_____

_____

_____

_____

_____

_____

Week 6 Takeaways

What key truths, principles, and/or insights will you take away from this week's experience?

_____

_____

_____

_____

_____

_____

Action Steps

What action steps will you prayerfully consider based on this week's experience? Remember, be patient to let God fully develop your action plan. Resist the urge to jump into action immediately. You will revisit these in week 8 to formalize a clear plan of action for leading the _DiscipleShift_ within your context.

_____

_____

_____

_____

_____

_____

Setup For Next Week

The final piece of the puzzle or cog in the wheel is Culture Change and Celebration. If we've been successfully building momentum through a careful process that shifts individuals and the church at large toward disciple-making, one thing remains. A change of culture is the destination toward which everything has been leading, and celebration of the goals and values identified are the fuel that keeps everyone moving together.

culture change and celebration

"Why do people get so excited for a football game, but they just sit there at a worship service?" Countless church leaders have asked this question. It is a valid concern and a fair contrast. Certainly, everyone readily admits that Christ is infinitely more worthy of our passion than any sporting event. Yet the truth is that football, especially college football, has built a very specific and clear culture over time. This culture of habits and behaviors is passed down and made permanent, cemented into the hearts and minds of people through celebration. But this is not a new phenomenon. Throughout biblical history, God's people have been instructed to commemorate and celebrate His work in their lives —from the Passover meal and Ebenezer stone to baptism and communion. This week we are going to examine the vital role of celebration and its impact on culture.

Day 1

WHY CELEBRATE?

In the early days of Real Life Ministries, one of the things Jim would talk about from the stage was home groups reaching out to families in the community outside the church. For instance, Jim would hear about a family that had suffered a serious tragedy. Jim would call home groups to make meals for them. Those meals made a big difference to the families. Anyone who has suffered a family loss knows it can be very difficult for the family to eat, much less think about preparing food. Making a meal for another family is a warm gesture, and the family in crisis feels supported and cared for.

Many of our first families came to the church because home groups had prepared meals for them. Jim would talk about onstage and regularly celebrate what home groups were doing to love their neighbors. The celebrations became normal behavior at the church and then part of the culture. Soon church leadership stopped asking the groups to do things. They began reaching out on their own. The celebration turned into culture, which became a value of anyone who is part of our church body.

Consider how many holidays or major events are observed in the United States. Some observed events don't even have a national or religious value to them—Ground Hog Day, Valentine's Day, Mother's Day, and so on. The culture observes them and responds accordingly with the behavior that matches the tradition of the culture. Government and community leaders don't spend a dollar on advertising, yet next April First, we will all plan pranks on others.

What do you do automatically with family, friends, or other relationships because of culture? (For example, a potluck third Thursday of the month, tailgating, hunting on the same day every year, and so forth.)

_____

_____

_____

_____

_____

_____

The more your church or ministry starts to move in the direction of the desired change, the more you'll need to intentionally celebrate. The more you celebrate in specifically talking about and praising behavior that leads to change, the more the church body will work to accomplish greater things. Culture is shaped by celebration. For example, consider relational environments for the purpose of discipleship. A component of healthy relational environments is caring for others. Making meals for other families is a tangible expression of caring for others. By celebrating the behavior, you are starting to shape culture in the direction of healthy change and a positive shift in your church.

With what tangible acts do you and others naturally respond when the following events occur?

St. Patrick's Day	_____	Black Friday	_____
April Fool's Day	_____	Arbor Day	_____
Halloween	_____	Flag Day	_____
Valentine's Day	_____	Thanksgiving	_____

All of your responses were originally shaped by celebration, and none of the responses have to be monitored, controlled, or dictated. The responses are a natural in our culture. A hundred years from now, most likely your answers will be true for your great-grandchildren.

Imagine leading a church that naturally behaved in ways that produced healthy relational environments. When you celebrate such actions your people naturally will repeat them.

What is your church already doing that leads to relational environments for discipleship? How will you celebrate those behaviors?

_____

_____

_____

_____

_____

_____

_____

Read Acts 2:42-47. Circle the Christians' tangible acts that led to a healthy church.

No wonder God added to their numbers daily! If your church environment is healthy and conducive to building disciples, your church will grow!

This week we are going to focus on celebrating the tangible behaviors that lead to healthy relational environments. Celebration is essential in building a culture that performs on its own.

They devoted themselves to the apostles' teaching and to fellowship, to the breaking of bread and to prayer. Everyone was filled with awe at the many wonders and signs performed by the apostles. All the believers were together and had everything in common. They sold property and possessions to give to anyone who had need. Every day they continued to meet together in the temple courts. They broke bread in their homes and ate together with glad and sincere hearts, praising God and enjoying the favor of all the people. And the Lord added to their number daily those who were being saved.

(Act 2:42-47)

Day 2

WHAT TO CELEBRATE

This entire workbook has been focused on you and your team leading healthy change in your church, specifically, shifting the culture of your church to one of discipleship. Let's assume that once you start putting these principles into action, you do everything well to this point. The church and your team will probably be experiencing some feeling of accomplishment.

Good for you! Here is a reality check, though, for you to consider: the church hasn't truly gone through a change unless the culture has changed and aligned. This is a lot harder than you think, and it may take years to see group norms conform.

Consider this: God wanted to free His people from slavery in Egypt. He could have just pulled them out and been done with it. After all, He is God. However, God wanted to lead change well and change the hearts of the people. One of the ways He did that was to accomplish some short-term goals and communicate the results. In this case He systematically demolished an Egyptian-god organizational chart and with each plague proved who He was for His people. He proved that only He was God as He knocked off each Egyptian god—starting at the bottom and working His way up—finally proving that He was greater and more powerful than anything in the Egyptian religious culture. After this incredible display of power and love, His people were finally removed from captivity. Freedom—at least for the Israelites!

Even then, the Israelites wanted to go back to Egypt and slavery. Bondage was what they were used to; it was their culture and it hadn't changed yet. Look at the following verses:

As Pharaoh approached, the Israelites looked up, and there were the Egyptians, marching after them. They were terrified and cried out to the Lord. They said to Moses, "Was it because there were no graves in Egypt that you brought us to the desert to die? What have you done to us by bringing us out of Egypt? Didn't we say to you in Egypt, 'Leave us alone; let us serve the Egyptians'? It would have been better for us to serve the Egyptians than to die in the desert!" . . . In the desert the whole community grumbled against Moses and Aaron. The Israelites said to them, "If only we had died by the Lord's hand in Egypt! There we sat around pots of meat and ate all the food we wanted, but you have brought us out into this desert to starve this entire assembly to death." . . . But the people were thirsty for water there, and they grumbled against Moses. They said, "Why did you bring us up out of Egypt to make us and our children and livestock die of thirst?" (Exodus 14:10-11; 16:2-3; 17:3)

God absolutely accomplished leading healthy change. He heard the cries of His people and responded to their plea for freedom. But when the Israelites got what they had begged for, they decided what they really wanted was to go back to something unhealthy and harmful rather than adapt to a new culture. People would rather stay where they know it is not as good than go to a place that is not as familiar.

What are some of the toughest habits you have had to quit?

_____

_____

_____
_____
_____
_____
_____

Maybe you are still struggling in bondage over certain behaviors or attitudes. When you think about stopping a bad habit, do you want to go "cold turkey" or would you rather gradually taper off the occurrences of your habit?

_____
_____
_____
_____
_____
_____
_____

The important takeaway from today is not for you to lose hope in leading healthy change in your church. Instead, put reality on the table and know that you are going to be in a battle for many years over changing culture. Some of your people will make the change faster than others. This relates to your answer on the last question. Some of the people changed their perception of the culture cold turkey, while others are slower and more methodical.

As we learned in yesterday's study, celebration is one very key way to start to change culture. There are undoubtedly events and habits that are already on the schedule that will keep people tied to the old culture. As you remove these items from the culture, slowly but surely the culture will begin to change. For instance, let's say your change toward relational small groups is working well and you have several new groups forming. Next month one of your local Bible teachers is going to have his quarterly gathering where he preaches verse by verse for the evening. People typically enjoy this time of Bible teaching and you always look forward to it as well. The problem is that it is not relational. People get information, but they aren't able to truly apply it without relationship and accountability. The solution is a compromise. You videotape the Bible teacher and then send DVDs to group leaders so people can discuss the teaching in their groups. Everyone receives the benefits without having to go all the way back into Egypt.

What scheduled events or celebrations in your church need to be eliminated or modified?

_____
_____
_____
_____
_____
_____
_____

You may feel as though we're drawing a line in the sand where a line isn't necessary. Isn't it okay to keep a few events to make people happy? The truth is you can't be moving toward freedom and celebrate captivity at the same time. If you are going to lead change, then go in that direction. Going back and forth only confuses the people you're leading.

HOW DO WE REMEMBER?

Day 3

Anyone who has lived in a small town for any period of time knows that the locals hardly ever use actual street names for reference. In order to get their bearings, people use land-marks—a rock, a sign, a prominent house or building. If you ask for directions, you'll hear something like this: "Turn left at the old Johnson house, and the Smiths live in the green house on the left-hand side just before the stop sign." In rural communities those directions are more effective than turn-by-turn navigation. It makes a person wonder, if all the landmarks were removed, could anyone navigate in their community?

In Joshua chapter 4 God commanded the Israelites who had finally made it into the Promised Land to set up a new landmark for future generations.

When the whole nation had finished crossing the Jordan, the Lord said to Joshua, "Choose twelve men from among the people, one from each tribe, and tell them to take up twelve stones from the middle of the Jordan, from right where the priests are standing, and carry them over with you and put them down at the place where you stay tonight."

So Joshua called together the twelve men he had appointed from the Israelites, one from each tribe, and said to them, "Go over before the ark of the Lord your God into the middle of the Jordan. Each of you is to take up a stone on his shoulder, according to the number of the tribes of the Israelites, to serve as a sign among you. In the future, when your children ask you, 'What do these stones mean?' tell them that the flow of the Jordan was cut off before the ark of the covenant of the Lord. When it crossed the Jordan, the waters of the Jordan were cut off. These stones are to be a memorial to the people of Israel forever."

So the Israelites did as Joshua commanded them. They took twelve stones from the middle of the Jordan, according to the number of the tribes of the Israelites, as the Lord had told Joshua; and they carried them over with them to their camp, where they put them down. Joshua set up the twelve stones that had been in the middle of the Jordan at the spot where the priests who carried the ark of the cov-enant had stood. And they are there to this day. (Joshua 4:1-9)

The stones were a physical reminder, a celebration of something the Lord had done through His people. Just like using buildings and other landmarks to give directions in small towns, these spiritual markers would be there to help the Israelites get their bearings and find their way.

What are spiritual markers for your personal journey with the Lord? What physical rep-resentations of those markers help you to remember spiritual truths?

_____

_____

_____

_____

_____

This week we are discussing the role and need for celebrations to change culture. A good thing to do before you celebrate is to take a picture or create a physical landmark for people to remember. Every time they see that picture in the lobby, they remember what the Lord did and they remember their response. It is amazing how various objects can trigger our memories.

Recently, I (Lance) attended a conference where they talked about increasing your memory. One of the tips they gave involved creating triggers to help you remember. For example, if you can't remember to take your pills, then think of something you always do about the time you are supposed to take the pills and link it with the action. I turn off this light before going to bed, now when I do I am going to ask myself, "Did I take my pills?"

What are some permanent, tangible things you can do to link to celebrations you've already planned? How will people see that and remember what they did and, more importantly, what they are supposed to do in the future?

The goal of these physical reminders is to anchor these new behaviors of the entire church culture. We know that when we personally or as a congregation have spiritual victories, Satan likes to attack; we are tested. We don't want our people, who have made healthy changes, to give the ground they have worked so hard to secure.

Even Jesus was led out into the desert to be tested after a big spiritual celebration. Read about the celebration Jesus had in the following verses.

> Then Jesus came from Galilee to the Jordan to be baptized by John. But John tried to deter him, saying, "I need to be baptized by you, and do you come to me?"
> Jesus replied, "Let it be so now; it is proper for us to do this to fulfill all righteousness." Then John consented.

As soon as Jesus was baptized, he went up out of the water. At that moment heaven was opened, and he saw the Spirit of God descending like a dove and alighting on him. And a voice from heaven said, "This is my Son, whom I love; with him I am well pleased." (Matthew 3:13-17)

Then the very next verse tells us what happened after this highpoint in Jesus's life: "Then Jesus was led by the Spirit into the wilderness to be tempted by the devil" (Matthew 4:1). Celebrations and intentional reminders can help people hold their ground when they start to doubt or life gets tough.

WHERE WILL YOU GO FROM HERE?

Day 4

When you were a child, did you ever try to play a game with a friend who kept changing the rules? Usually the rules changed to give your friend a decided advantage. That scenario is never very much fun. As adults, when we play a new game the first thing we ask is usually "What are the rules and how do I win?"

We all want to win. It is part of what motivates us and helps us make decisions. And there most certainly would not be practice if winning weren't attached to it somehow.

Being a member of a church is no different. We want to know how to win in our environment—what gets recognition, what gets respect, what are we trying to do together to win! We talk with many church leaders, and they're always frustrated with the congregation for not wanting to be more involved and vested. In many cases the leadership has unintentionally not communicated the vision, mission, and purpose to the church. Therefore, the congregation doesn't know how to win and consequently doesn't know how to participate.

Assuming that the congregation is clear on the win, the mission, and vision of your church, we will focus on a common omission in communication: tying information to the win.

Step #1: Tying Information to the Win

Coaches are usually quite skilled at tying information to the win. They say things like "The reason we're doing all these push-ups is to get you in better shape than your opponent. If you're in better shape, we will win." In football or any other sport or game, how to win is clearly communicated. The person or team that has a better score wins. What an athlete does in August on the practice field in the heat of two-a-days matters in October during a game.

In church we participate in many activities. The entire congregation has a routine, a dance, that happens weekly. This person makes coffee, another member greets. Others hand out bulletins, teach, preach, and so forth. If leadership was intentional and consistent with how people's activities in the church impacted the win, think how encouraged they would be. They would start to make connections between their activity and the greater impact of the church. Individuals would not only be motivated in their ministry, they would also have freedom to create and grow in that ministry. That is the impact on the individual when they hear how they are impacting the overall church win by their actions. The entire congregation is moved, and a winning culture forms when activities get tied to the win.

Here is what tying information to the win looks like in a church setting. A leader makes an announcement at some point during the service: "We are going to celebrate with a baptism after the sermon today. We all get to celebrate together, but it was really what [name of individual] did when she shared Christ with [name]. She went out of her way to look for an opportunity, and now we all can celebrate! She was scared, but she fought through that fear. That is how we can see our mission here at [name of church] happen."

There is power in winning! It raises spirits and builds culture quickly because we all want to be a part of something that is larger than ourselves. We want to win.

Even bad news or discomfort can be communicated as a win as it ties back to overall mission of the church. For example, "Isn't it great how you had to walk all that way into church this morning because all of the parking spots close to the building were already taken? The parking lot is filling up because you are being the church!" Even new people who had trouble getting into the building would be happy about their poor experience after hearing that.

The following exercise will help get you into the habit of tying information to the mission of the church. Write the brief details of a story or an announcement that you know you have to communicate to the congregation, and then tie it to the vision of the church.

Information Piece   Tie In

_____   _____
_____   _____
_____   _____
_____   _____
_____   _____
_____   _____
_____   _____

Step #2: Where and When to Communicate the Win

Now that we are seeing opportunities for motivating and leading the church through this form of communication, we need to look for as many environments as we can in which to send it. Chances are there are many opportunities that leadership is not using to communicate the win. First, we will look at existing forms of communication that the church already uses. Then we will brainstorm ways leadership could start to create new opportunities.

How does your leadership communicate with the congregation?

_____
_____
_____
_____
_____
_____

Before you start brainstorming, here are a few suggestions to get you started: individual leadership meetings, social media, sermon illustrations, church events. When you start to look for new opportunities, you'll be amazed at how many will appear.

How can leadership change or create areas to communicate what a win is for the congregation?

_____

_____

_____

_____

_____

_____

_____

The future is wide open when a church culture understands what winning looks like. People you didn't think were leaders will start to contribute in new ways. Ideas and motivation will seem to erupt spontaneously when individuals understand what a win is.

Day 5

REVIEW AND GROUP DISCUSSION

Pray
Begin your time together in prayer.

Scripture
Today's reading is lengthier, but the detail is important.
Choose at least two people to read Nehemiah 8 and 12:27-43.

Key Points
- Chapter 8 has been read before (during week 2), but it is a critical point to see from another perspective this week.
- (8:1) As we saw before in chapter 8, the people gathered together as one. They were united, no longer divided and scattered.
- (8:1-4) God's Word was central, revered, and obeyed. The authority of God was what united the community.
- (8:5-8) Wise leadership is important, but its primary objective is to point people back to God's Word and to make clear the meaning and appropriate response.
- (8:9-10) Rallying the people was not a matter of beating them up with guilt and commands, but reminding them of God's gracious love and mercy.
- (8:11-18) Celebrating the work of God in the life of His people has always been central. The community of God has always revolved around key celebrations.
- (12:27-43) Within the elaborate detail given to the description of the celebration in chapters 8 and 12 are climactic moments for the sweeping change led by Nehemiah out of conviction according to God's Word. A vital part in culture change and a vibrant community is celebration. It is not enough to merely do the work. God's people are expected to celebrate—for their own sake (morale), for the world's sake (witness, 12:43), and for God's sake (glorifying Him with praise).

Scripture focuses on corporate commitment, change, and celebration of God's work. That is what wakes people up in the morning ready to be on a mission with God. If we are truly going to lead a shift in culture, we must celebrate.

The Week in Review
Discuss the major points and questions of each day, revisiting anything you may have marked throughout the week for group discussion. Share honestly about where God is challenging and encouraging you. Make sure your group environment is one of mutual respect, tempering observations and responses with grace. Time will not allow you to discuss all the questions, but visit the milestones and make sure each group member has an opportunity to offer input.

Day 1: Why celebrate?
Day 2: What to celebrate
Day 3: How do we remember?
Day 4: Where will you go from here?

Personal "Shifts" As a Disciple

What is God teaching you about Himself? About yourself? About your church?

_____
_____
_____
_____
_____
_____

Week 7 Takeaways

What key truths, principles, and/or insights will you take away from this week's experience?

_____
_____
_____
_____
_____
_____
_____
_____

Action Steps

What action steps will you prayerfully consider based on this week's experience? Remember, be patient to let God fully develop your action plan. Resist the urge to jump into action immediately. You will revisit these in week 8 to formalize a clear plan of action for leading the *DiscipleShift* within your context.

_____
_____
_____
_____
_____
_____

Setup For Next Week

This is the most important part of the entire process. The past seven weeks have been working through principles and practices for leading the DiscipleShift. Each week you have been encouraged to reflect on personal shifts, takeaways, and possible action steps. You have also been reminded to prayerfully and patiently wait to implement any of the changes you may be eager to get rolling. This coming week you will walk back through the journey and finally piece everything together, viewing it all through a holistic lens to see the big picture and the practical steps needed in your own context. You will be guided through a review process and formulate an action plan proposal. Next week when you gather again as a group, we will synthesize all the findings for your church leadership into a master plan for leading the DiscipleShift.

leading the discipleShift action plan

This final week is designed to pull all the pieces together and give you and your team an agreed-upon action plan for becoming a disciple-making church.

This is the most important part of the entire process. The past seven weeks have been working through principles and practices for leading the *DiscipleShift*. Each week you have been encouraged to reflect on personal shifts, takeaways, and possible action steps. You have also been reminded to prayerfully and patiently wait to implement any of the changes you may be eager to get rolling.

This week you will walk back through the journey and finally piece everything together, viewing it all through a holistic lens to see the big picture and the practical steps needed in your own context. You will be guided through a review process and formulate an action plan proposal. On day 5, when you gather again as a group, you will synthesize all the findings for your church leadership into a master plan for leading the *DiscipleShift*.

Finish strong!

Day 1

REVIEW AND REFLECT

Week 1: Foundational Definitions
Review

Before a leadership team can lead a church body through change, a common goal must be established. Week 1 helped you to focus on not only a clear goal, but also the right goal. To effectively lead change in the church, your leadership team was challenged to define terms the same way, using the same words. In week 1 you worked through such key concepts as the purpose of the church and the definition of a disciple, and you took a deeper look at relationship.

Reflect

Take a moment to reflect on your small group time at the end of week 1. Review your answers and then answer the following questions:

1. How has God changed your view of His purpose for His church?

2. How has your perspective on the role of relationships changed, and how do you believe relationships will impact change?

3. What action step(s) did you identify in week 1 to prayerfully consider for week 8?

Week 2: Five Components and Shifts in Disciple-Making

Review

To hit a target you must set your sights on the target. Week 2 challenged you to break down discipleship into individual components. The goal of this week was to outline those components to help your leadership team understand what you are shifting the church toward. Much like Nehemiah, leadership must know what the end goal is in order to effectively lead change. These five components help create a common direction and provide clarity to creating a healthy church that makes healthy disciples.

Reflect

Take a moment to reflect on your small group time at the end of week 2. Review your answers and then answer the following questions:

1. In what ways were you challenged to be more intentional as a leader, and where has God grown you in the area of intentional leadership?

2. How has God grown the team in your relational connection, and how do you believe this will help your overall alignment?

3. Which of the five shifts did you and the group identify with most? Why?

4. Which of the five shifts do you feel needs to be addressed immediately, and which do you believe could wait? Why?

_____

_____

_____

_____

_____

_____

5. What action step(s) did you identify in week 2 to prayerfully consider for week 8?

_____

_____

_____

_____

_____

Week 3: Being a Leader Who Makes God Proud
Review

Understanding your impact on the environment becomes vital when leading change. In week 3 you spent time evaluating and investigating the impact of your leadership on the culture of the church. As a courageous leader, you looked in the mirror, asked some hard questions, and made an honest evaluation. As a group you looked for gaps that needed to be filled in and how you could clarify the vision for where God was leading you.

Reflect

Take a moment to reflect on your small group time at the end of week 3. Review your answers and then answer the following questions:

1. When you evaluated the impact of your leadership on the current church environment, what did God teach you about yourself?

_____

_____

_____

_____

_____

2. In day 3 of week 3 you looked at the gaps in your ministry. What did you find? How will you apply this new understanding to leading change?

_____

_____

_____
_____
_____
_____
_____

3. What action step(s) did you identify in week 3 to prayerfully consider for week 8?

_____
_____
_____
_____
_____
_____

Week 4: Healthy Tension and Building Support (Team, Tension, and Communication)
Review

In week 5 you began to make the shift. Looking back, you can see that you moved from a more personal perspective on your leadership and your personal ownership to philosophical concepts to help you get others onboard. Inviting people onto your team and rallying them is vital to changing your church direction and culture. Week 4 helped you move from more big-picture organizational concepts to actual investment in those who will help execute the change in your church.

Reflect

Take a moment to reflect on your small group time at the end of week 4. Review your answers and then answer the following questions.

1. What has the Lord taught you about team-building?

_____
_____
_____
_____
_____
_____

2. When it comes to building the team that will help implement change in your church, why is the team-building process so vital to healthy change?

_____
_____
_____
_____
_____

3. What action step(s) did you identify in week 4 to prayerfully consider for week 8?

Week 5: Overcoming Obstacles
Review

Almost every obstacle in a church is tied to a person. One Christian leader once said, "Church would be so much easier if it were not for the people." In week 5 you were challenged to identify and overcome the obstacles you would face when implementing change. This very practical chapter should have helped you develop some steps to overcoming those obstacles and gain some relational skills and ideas to help lead your people.

Reflect

Take a moment to reflect on your small group time at the end of week 5. Review your answers and then answer the following questions:

1. What obstacles stand out as most obvious? What is your plan to tackle those?

2. What is God teaching you about your leadership and taking on obstacles? How is He leading you to grow?

3. What action step(s) did you identify in week 5 to prayerfully consider for week 8?

_____

Week 6: SMART Goals and Momentum
Review

You have begun working through recruiting, building, and aligning a team. In week 6 you looked at healthy goal setting, how to build momentum with your newly recruited team, and how vital these components are to effectively leading change. There has to be momentum to sustain change and carry the team forward.

Reflect

Take a moment to reflect on your small group time at the end of week 6. Review your answers and then answer the following questions:

1. What concerns or doubts surfaced as your small group processed the concepts of setting goals and building momentum?

_____

2. What ideas did you discuss to build momentum? How do you see these ideas positively impacting your church culture?

_____

3. What action step(s) did you identify in week 6 to prayerfully consider for week 8?

_____

Week 7: Culture Change and Celebration
Review

You made it! Week 7 challenged you to look at ways to celebrate and maintain this new healthy direction. Much like the Israelites did in the Old Testament, we wanted you to understand the importance of spiritual markers. To uphold the changes you will make, leadership teams must celebrate the wins. This helps create a healthy culture that constantly and consistently reviews God's work in the lives of those in your church body.

Reflect

Take a moment to reflect on your small group time at the end of week 7. Review your answers and then answer the following questions:

1. How will you celebrate the successes as you lead change?

_____

_____

_____

_____

_____

_____

2. What is the future for your church? Take a moment to write a possible future scenario that would describe your church body truly "winning."

_____

_____

_____

_____

_____

_____

3. What action step(s) did you identify in week 7 to prayerfully consider for week 8?

_____

_____

_____

_____

_____

DEVELOPING YOUR ACTION PLAN (PART 1)

Day 2

Being a Disciple-Maker of Jesus, Developing a Disciple-Making Church of Jesus

During today's exercise you are going to choose actions steps that you are committed to completing. The purpose of this exercise is to give you some clear next steps to help you lead yourself, your team, and your church toward becoming a better disciple-making church.

Today, read through all of the suggested steps and then select twenty individual action steps to complete. Tomorrow, on day 3, you will write those twenty steps on and prioritize them, so don't get caught up today in ranking them as you go.

On day 4 you will be choosing seven of your twenty steps that you feel each person in your group should also be willing to do. Those will become your seven team/corporate action steps that you will present to your group on day 5. (We recommend two to four hours to complete the activities on day 5.)

Note: Please feel free to add any additional steps you would like to complete that are not listed. These may include, but are not limited to, any steps you reviewed yesterday—possible action steps you identified and have been praying over from the weekly exercises.

Action Steps for Becoming a Disciple-Maker of Jesus

_____ I will assess where I am spiritually and share that information with two other people.

Names: _____

_____ I will commit to being discipled/equipped/apprenticed _____ hours each week.

_____ I will seek out and ask another person to disciple me.

Identify three people: _____

_____

Choose one: _____

_____ I will disciple another person toward Jesus by doing the following:

> Seeking out and relationally investing in being their friend.
> Helping them recognize how God has gifted them.
> Encourage their walk with the Lord, modeling for them reading, praying, etc.
> Invite them over for dinner and express interest in what God is doing in their life.
> Call and text them during the day to let them know what their friendship means to me.

_____ I will share with them my struggles and ask for some godly advice.

_____ I am committed to be in a weekly small group. If one is not available, I will start one.

_____ I am committed to leading people toward making disciples of Jesus in a positive way.

_____ I am committed to building a Christ-centered environment, focusing on what God is doing around me and helping others do the same. I will not focus on what is broken and not working, but rather be part of the solution. I will help others around me see what God is doing and encourage them in their walk. I will humbly ask for input on how to better lead. I will identify three relational tensions I have not worked out with others, and I commit to the Lord that I will work them out. First, I will pray about the matter, and then I will initiate a conversation with the person.

Relational tension #1 _____
Relational tension #2 _____
Relational tension #3 _____

_____ I am committed to do what the Lord has commanded me to do: make disciples of Jesus.

_____ I am committed to helping another group get started using this workbook.

_____ I am committed to finding out if the people around me have a real relationship with the Lord by:
　　　Asking if and how they accepted Jesus,
　　　Making listening to them a priority by making time for them,
　　　Being genuinely curious about how they came to know the Lord,
　　　Being genuinely curious about how they view the church and God,
　　　Thanking God for the opportunity to hear another person's "story."

_____ I am committed to praying the following (or something close to it) every morning:
"Lord, give me a heart to love Your people better. Help me listen to Your people with a genuine, caring heart. Help me model what I am asking or expecting others around me to do."
_____ I will contact the absentees this week and for the next four weeks.

_____ I will ask for the names of the visitors and contact one person this week.

_____ I will define what it means to be a disciple of Jesus and reflect on how I am walking that out by (date) _____.

_____ I will discover the needs of the people outside the church in my community.

_____ I will be a more relational leader by having fun with three co-workers.

Names: _____

Activity: _____

Completion date: _____

_____ I will ask five people what they feel the purpose of the church is. Then I will reflect on the journey God took me on to help bring clarity regarding the church's purpose.

Names: _____

_____ I will change my schedule to leave more margin for relational discipleship.

The changes I will make include _____

_____

_____

_____

_____ I will commit to pray weekly with my team this prayer (or one like it):

"Lord, help me further Your kingdom by being a lover of You and your people. Help me make relationship with You and others a top priority. Lord, please give me Your grace and Your wisdom to make the necessary changes so my life reflects what You care about. Amen."

_____ I will ask others in my family to describe what the environment is like with me and without me.

_____ I will ask my co-workers to describe the environment I create around me.

_____ I will ask my friends to describe what it's like to be in relationship with me.

_____ I will be intentionally more relational with my team. To do so, I will make the following changes: _____

_____

_____

_____

_____

_____ I will commit to pray weekly with my team this prayer (or one like it):

_____ I will commit to pray weekly with my team this prayer (or one like it):

_____ I will share with the people around me the journey the Lord has taken me on regarding making disciples of Jesus.

_____ I will share with others around me the conviction I have regarding making disciples of Jesus.

_____ I will brainstorm with the team ways we could make more of an impact in our community.

_____ I will help lead others to a unified purpose of the church and common definition of a disciple.

_____ I will commit to learning how to better lead someone to the Lord, by talking with _____, who is great at leading people to the Lord, by (date) _____.

_____ I will help the leadership reach an agreement on the purpose of the church (to make disciples of Jesus).

_____ I will create relational environments within my office and church building.

_____ I will lead my team into an agreement on a definition of a disciple.

_____ I am committed to help our entire congregation understand that they are to be making disciples of Jesus. I will brainstorm with my group some ideas on how to bring this about.

_____ I will evaluate my budget in comparison to the purpose of the church.

_____ I will develop a leadership communication plan that encourages the congregation toward making disciples.

_____ I am willing to voice my thoughts and concerns but will support the final decisions of the leadership.

_____ I will improve our membership covenant content and process to help our people know what we believe.

_____ I am willing to participate in solving problems in the church weekly.

_____ I am willing to give to the Lord through the ministry of this church _____ % of my income.

_____ I am willing to faithfully attend weekly services.

_____ I am willing to tithe.

_____ I will develop a firm grasp of the discipleship process.

_____ I will write out what being in relationship with me means. Then I will read what I've written to those on my team to help others better understand me and to value relationship as a priority in my life.

_____ I will intentionally pursue two people to develop a real relationship with them.

Names: _____

_____

_____ I will create a list of what I expect from others in a relationship and then model those expectations.

_____ I will reflect on the environment I have created in my area of influence, describe it on paper, and share my findings with two people.

Names: _____

_____ I will ask two people, "What do I do well as a leader?" and "What do I need to improve on as a leader?"

Names: _____

_____ I will talk to others in the church to discover (without judging) where they are in the discipleship process.

_____ I will ask my team in a genuine way about their personal understanding of the purpose of the church.

_____ I will read God's Word daily and intentionally look for the various relational aspects of His Word.

_____ I will write a paragraph for each person on my team that relates how I see each one making disciples of Jesus.

_____ I will list three ways our communication could be better aligned to making disciples of Jesus:

1. _____
2. _____
3. _____

_____ I will find out what each team member is doing to challenge himself or herself spiritually.

_____ I will brainstorm ways my team can help align the church to make disciples.

_____ I will commit to review our staff and volunteers to determine if any should be moved or hired to align with discipleship.

_____ I will make a list of key influencers who could, if they got on board with making disciples of Jesus, could help us turn this ship.

_____ I will brainstorm with my group ways to get the identified influencers on board with making disciples the way Jesus did.

_____ I will review the church budget and compare it to the values of making disciples of Jesus.

_____ I will brainstorm ways I can help align the church theologically by helping our staff and key volunteers be able to explain to a new person what we believe theologically and why.

_____ I will rally the team to brainstorm possible ways to help our entire church understand the discipleship process and their roles in it, starting with our small group leaders (if we have them).

_____ I will identify the relational environments that the church is already a part of in the community.

_____ I will list various outreach events we could do with the community to create a relational environment for discipleship.

_____ I will help train small group leaders to be disciple-makers of Jesus. This will include helping those leaders understand the disciple-making process and that they are disciple-makers no matter where they are.

_____ I will help other key influencers understand they are to make disciples of Jesus. That will include helping them see how Jesus did it.

_____ I am committed to helping move "equipping" out of classroom and into relational environments.

_____ I will sign up for the two-day *DisciplShift* training through Real Life Ministries (www.reallifeministries.com).

_____ I will intentionally encourage others around me start to minister to others every week.

_____ I will ask the Lord daily to help me focus on the people more than on the tasks.

_____ I will shape my daily ministry activities to be more relationally relevant by changing the following three things:

1. _____
2. _____
3. _____

_____ I will ask my team to consider the last time they were really stretched relationally.

_____ I will evaluate each team's ministry to see if it is more program than purpose.

_____ I will talk with my team about making disciples and gauge their level of commitment.

_____ I will talk with my team about ways we could better equip others for making disciples.

_____ I will ask my team how they feel they are doing with making disciples and why.

_____ I will take ownership of not equipping my team to make disciples of Jesus.

_____ I will communicate kingdom win stories of making disciples weekly.

_____ I will look for new leaders, invite them into a disciple-making journey, and begin to equip them for ministry by relationally investing in them and allowing them to do something for the church.

_____ I will change how we evaluate and measure ministry success. This evaluation will include but not be limited to making disciples of Jesus, creating places for others to get involved, putting relationships first, having a discipleship process, having small-group leaders who reach the lost and care for their people.

_____ I will ask for feedback from the groups I am leading on how I ampersonally impacting the environment both positively and negatively.

_____ I will increase the amount of intentionality I am placing on celebrating when I communicate.

_____ I will talk with the team corporately and individually about the positive and negative impact they are having.

_____ I will ask the team if they understand what it looks like to win in this ministry.

_____ I will ask each person on the team to invite feedback about how they are leading.

_____ I will ask the team to take an honest look at how it is influencing the rest of the church.

_____ I will ask the team for specific changes they could make to their ministry that would align better to making disciples.

_____ I will communicate with people who are making it difficult to make disciples because of their consistent negativity.

_____ I will ask the team to help me evaluate the church's current impact on the community.

_____ I will align or discontinue ministries that are a hobby and not focused on making disciples of Jesus.

_____ I am committed to helping the church understand what a win is and what their roles are.

_____ I will ask the team what skill set and personality would be a good fit and would fill a need on the team.

_____ I will make changes in the structure of the team to allow for new people.

_____ I will invite people personally to my team to help.

_____ I will evaluate my past actions regarding leading change. If I have not done it well in the past, I will be open to the Holy Spirit's leading me to apologize and ask for forgiveness.

_____ I will listen to people's hearts when communicating.

_____ I will personally brainstorm hurdles I can see to leading this change and potential solutions.

_____ I will evaluate myself and the team to see if there are other people we need to bring onto the team to help in leading this change.

_____ I will encourage members of the team.

_____ I will be intentional in meetings about verbally expressing what is going on inside of me as we discuss leading change.

_____ I will talk to the team about potential hurdles they see to successfully leading change. We will list them and discuss possible relational solutions to each hurdle.

_____ I will have the team brainstorm ways that they will hold each other accountable to continually put people ahead of tasks.

_____ I will communicate with church leadership the progress and pitfalls.

_____ I will talk with the team on how to have big-picture conversations with key volunteers.

_____ I will communicate to the church the team's goals and boundaries and what that means to the congregation.

_____ I will encourage the church body to pray for the team.

_____ I will preach several sermon series on church unity and the value of relationships.

_____ I will intentionally communicate to others around me what God is showing me about disciple-making.

_____ I will make a SMART goal for myself and evaluate the results.

_____ I will be more positive and look for things that are going well to communicate to others.

_____ I will work with the team on setting long-term ministry goals that have a unified vision.

_____ I will brainstorm with the team for ways to increase momentum in our ministry.

_____ I will make SMART goals for my ministry team.

_____ I will brainstorm with my team potential short-term-win stories.

_____ I will do my part of getting people on board with making disciples and ask them to do the same with their relationships.

_____ I will have the team talk to people outside of the ministry about all the great things that are happening.

_____ I will celebrate short-term wins in multiple ways.

_____ I will use personal testimonies of life change to help people better understand the big picture.

_____ I will communicate to the church long-term goals.

_____ I will take frequent breaks to look at the big picture.

_____ I will look at events in my life that have led up to making this change.

_____ I will pace myself and the people around me.

_____ I will make sure what we are communicating aligns with our goals.

_____ I will recognize that when I am tired of talking about the changes that means we are just getting started.

_____ I will make sure each ministry aligns with the vision. _____ I will make sure everyone on the team is moving together toward change at the same pace.

_____ I will have discussions with the team about this change being a marathon and not a sprint.

_____ I will make sure the team is looking at the bigger picture and not getting hung up in the small stuff.

_____ I will talk with the team about the culture changing to see if they agree.

_____ I will communicate with the congregation win stories that align with the vision.

_____ I will communicate with the church about the big picture and how we are going to align with it.

_____ I will celebrate what the Lord is doing in His church regarding life change.

_____ I will celebrate the little wins.

_____ I will celebrate what God is doing in my relationships with my family, friends, and co-workers.

DEVELOPING YOUR ACTION PLAN (PART 2)

Day 3

Using the twenty steps you selected yesterday, fill in the following chart with your personal action plan. Don't worry about writing them down in the "correct" order to begin with—you will further refine your list tomorrow. Today, simply consolidate your list, evaluate and number any steps needing to come in a particular sequence, and continue praying for wisdom in the process.

Step #	Personal Action Step

Day 4

CHOOSING GROUP ACTION STEPS

Great job! You have completed selecting twenty action steps that you are personally committed to accomplishing for the purpose of becoming a disciple-making church. Write your sequential action steps, in order, using the space below. (While rewriting these steps each day may feel redundant, each step refines clarity and reinforces the individual steps and the unified process.) Then begin to fill out the anticipated impact each action step will have on you, others, and the kingdom. (You will be sharing this with your group on day 5.)

Now write the time frame you feel is best suited for that next step to be accomplished. It should be realistic yet somewhat challenging. Also, keep in mind the variables—your current culture, availability of people, and so forth.

Selected action steps	Time required to accomplish this step (personally)	Time required to accomplish this step (as a team)

Next, identify a person in your group whom you would like to ask to be your accountability and encouraging partner to help celebrate as you complete your next steps. (You will be asking the person on day 5.)

Name: _____

Finally, choose seven of the twenty action steps that you feel the team should also complete to help propel your church to be a disciple-making church. (You may choose to put a star in the left margin next to steps to propose for your team.) Then use the final column to estimate a time frame you feel it will take to complete each of those seven action steps.

Be prepared to discuss these action steps and timeframes with your group.

Anticipated impact on myself, others, and the kingdom

Day 5

SHARING STEPS AND BUILDING YOUR GROUP ACTION PLAN

The purpose of today's group meeting is to realize that God is doing something with your group. You all have invested lots of time energy into this study for the purpose of furthering His kingdom. As you listen to your teammates share with you what they are committed to tackling for next steps, please encourage them and celebrate where God has taken this group and each person in the group.

After each person shares his or her next steps, we suggest you celebrate, encourage, and thank the person for being willing to tackle those steps and for being willing to lead through the DiscipleShift.

When everyone has shared his or her personal and group next steps, you will need to compile and build your team's unified action steps. This will take some discussion to land on seven action steps the group agrees to complete.

Before you begin, you will need a way to visually capture each person's group action steps. We suggest using a whiteboard, chalkboard, large screen display of some sort. As you accumulate more and more action steps it will become more important to be able to see all of them so you and your group can narrow down the list to seven.

The following steps will help take you through this process smoothly.

Step 1

Begin by having each person read aloud ten of the twenty individual action steps and the anticipated impact for each one. (We suggest ten only because of the time factor. If you have more time you can share more steps.)

Step 2

After each person has completed sharing their steps, take a moment to encourage him or her, celebrate the person's commitment, and thank God for that person being on His team, your team.

Step 3

Have each person share the seven action steps selected for your group and the anticipated impact of each one. Don't share why you selected that action step for the group; you will be doing that later. (The person who is recording the steps should change the pronoun from "I" to "we" at this point in the list.)

Step 4

Once all the action steps have been shared, each person should tell who they chose for an accountability/encouraging partner.

Step 5

Take time to pray for clarity and godly direction in your discussion. Ask God for discernment and direction to build His church, to model loving Him and the people He has put in your lives.

Step 6

Narrow down the choices for your seven corporate action steps. Start by eliminating duplicates. Then give each person the opportunity to share why they chose the steps they did. Make sure each person is heard and valued.

Once you have your seven steps, don't forget to record your list so one person can type it and send it out to group members. You can also use the chart on the following page keep a record here in your own book of the agreed actions steps. Be sure someone is clearly identified as the one to officially communicate with your team the plan of action for leading the *DiscipleShift* in your own context.

Step 7

Focus on each action step and ask, "How do we accomplish this? What is our first step? What is our second step?" and so on. (If you're running short on time, step 7 can be worked out in a follow-up meeting.)

Before you end your meeting, determine accountability partners and give time for the partners to decide when, how often, and where they will meet.

Final Words

Now that you've finished this workbook, we would like to pray for you and your group. Even though we are not with you in person, we want you to know our hearts.

Lord, thank You for the opportunity to write this workbook, and thank You for these people who care enough about Your kingdom to go through it. We lift up this group to You and ask that You walk beside them and encourage them. We pray, Lord, that they would lean on You for understanding and guidance. Use these folks in a mighty way to further Your kingdom. Make their time together special. May they bathe in Your joy and look upon this time as an adventure that You are leading. Thank You for the opportunity to serve you in different places yet with the same goal—to make disciples of Jesus. In His name, Amen.

To your group,

Thank you for your willingness to press forward and fight the right fights. Being a disciple-making church that reflects what Jesus cares about is worth fighting for. Thank you for your willingness to make a difference in your church. And thank you for going on this journey with us.

Lance, Luke, and Brandon

Leading the DiscipleShift Action Plan

Action Steps	How It Is Accomplished	Time

Date_____

Church/Ministry Name _____

Names of leaders present _____

_____

_____

_____

_____

_____

_____

_____

_____

ABOUT THE AUTHORS

Brandon Guindon is a coauthor of Real-Life Discipleship Training Manual and former executive pastor at Real Life Ministries in Post Falls, Idaho. He currently serves as the Director of Spiritual Formation and Global Leadership at the Metropolitan Baptist Church in Houston, Texas. He, along with his team, pioneered the small-groups ministry at Real Life. His passion and privilege for the past thirteen years has been to teach and train leaders from both the local and global church in how to make disciples through small groups. Brandon holds an MA in Church Leadership from Hope International University. He and his wife, Amber, have four children.

Lance Wigton, Director of Church Planting for Real Life Ministries, was a part of the original home group that planted Real Life. Since his time on staff, the church has grown into one of the largest in the United States. Nestled in the heart of north Idaho, Real Life Ministries has achieved megachurch status with 8,000 people in weekly attendance in a very rural area. (The entire county has less than 100,000 people.) Along with the original campus, in Post Falls RLM has planted six other churches that are all exceeding the national church averages of attendance and baptisms. Lance has been on staff at Real Life Ministries for more than twelve years and lives in Post Falls, with his wife of twenty-three years, Angie, and their three lovely daughters: Meghan, 22; Abbie, 20; and Sofie, 17.

Luke Yetter is an Executive Pastor at Real Life Ministries, and is the Executive Director of the Relational Discipleship Network. He oversees the RLM Church Planters, and helped develop the Real Life Ministries *DiscipleShift* training program, which provides Relational Discipleship training on local, regional, national and international levels. He has been with Real Life Ministries for the past 11 years. He attended both North Idaho College and Eastern Washington University where he majored in Billiards and Ping Pong. He was the founder and CEO of a national corporation, Critical Power. He sold the company after 11 years to go into full-time ministry. Luke is married to his wife Casey and they have 3 children. He loves spending time with his family, teaching his kids to fish and enjoy the outdoors. He can often be found snowmobiling or biking through the woods of North Idaho with his family.